The Privilege of Aging

Portraits of Twelve Jewish Women

Also by Patricia Gottlieb Shapiro

Coming Home To Yourself: Eighteen Wise Women Reflect on Their Journeys

Yoga For Women At Midlife & Beyond: A Home Companion

Heart To Heart: Deepening Women's Friendships at Midlife

My Turn: Women's Search for Self After the Children Leave

Always My Child: A Parent's Guide to Understanding Your Gay, Lesbian, Bisexual, Transgendered or Questioning Son or Daughter (with coauthor)

A Parent's Guide To Childhood And Adolescent Depression

Women, Mentors & Success (with coauthor)

Caring For The Mentally Ill

The Privilege of Aging

Portraits of Twelve Jewish Women

Patricia Gottlieb Shapiro

Gaon Books
www.gaonbooks.com

For permissions, group pricing, and other information contact
Gaon Books
P.O. Box 23924
Santa Fe, NM 87502
or write (gaonbooks@gmail.com).

Manufactured in the United States of America.
 The paper used in this publication is acid free and meets all ANSI (American National Standards for Information Sciences) standards for archival quality paper. All wood product components used in this book are Sustainable Forest Initiative (SFI) certified.

Library of Congress Cataloging-in-Publication Data

Shapiro, Patricia Gottlieb.
 The privilege of aging : portraits of twelve Jewish women / Patricia Gottlieb Shapiro, M.S.W.
 pages cm
 Includes bibliographical references.
 ISBN 978-1-935604-52-5 (pbk. : alk. paper) -- ISBN 978-1-935604-53-2 (ebook)
 1. Older women--United States. 2. Jewish women--United States. 3. Aging--United States--Psychological aspects. I. Title.
 HQ1064.U5S515 2013
 305.26'20973--dc23
 2013011676

Cover and interior photographs are by Patricia Gottlieb Shapiro or by friends and family of the subjects.

Contents

"With age comes wisdom, and length of days brings understanding."

--Job 12:20

Acknowledgments

So MANY PEOPLE HAVE CONTRIBUTED TO MAKE this book a reality and have supported and encouraged me in the long book-making process.

Early on, I knew I wanted to write about older women's lives, but I did not have a direction. One day I was telling my mentor Sonia Nelson that I was looking for a focus to help me explore women's earlier lives as well as one that was pertinent for them as older women. Without skipping a beat, she responded, "*Parinama*." *Parinama* is Sanskrit for transformation and change and is the one thing that is constant in all of our lives. Examining the women's response to transitions turned out to be an ideal way to coax out the subtleties of their resilience and show the patterns and themes throughout their lives. Thank you, Sonia.

I am grateful for the many friends, acquaintances, family members and colleagues who suggested people for me to interview for this book. They did not all materialize into participants. I do want to thank individually those whose recommendations did result in the women becoming a part of this book. They are Lynn Altshul, Margo Bachman, Nicolai Bachman, Ellen Bartoldus, Norma Bolden, Sue Cohen Brown, Joyce Friedman, Ron Duncan Hart, Pat Kutay, Susan and Michael Norman, Sonia Nelson, and Nurit Patt.

I am most appreciative for the twelve women who participated in the book. These women come from a generation that is not always comfortable talking about the personal aspects of their lives and yet they willingly and openly shared with me some of their most challenging and private moments. It was an honor to get to know them and gain a better understanding of their desire to continue growing and developing as they age.

For their thoughtful reading of my manuscript and for their insightful and sensitive comments, I want to thank Martha Jablow and Rosemary Thompson. It continues to be a pleasure to work with my publisher, Ron Duncan Hart of Gaon Books. He was very interested in this project from the start and has been completely committed to the book throughout. I also want to thank Gloria Abella Ballen for her creative work on the art and design of the book.

Lastly, I am most appreciative of my close friends and family who continue to be a constant source of support and encouragement for my writing and for me. A special thanks goes to my husband Dick whose steadfast love day in and day out has sustained me and inspired me to continue growing and to follow my dreams.

Introduction

O**N THESE PAGES, YOU WILL MEET TWELVE** women from all parts of the country, women with different lifestyles, experiences, and economic backgrounds. You will read about the courage and bravery of a Holocaust survivor, the strength of a teacher to stand up for equal rights for women, the determination of an artist to nurture a long-term relationship.

These women have three things in common: their age—they are all over seventy-five years old—their vitality in coping with the challenges that accompany aging, and their connection to Judaism.

These women are aging well. They lead active, vibrant lives. Their lifelong journeys reveal how their earlier years prepared them for life as older women and how they learned from those experiences. My goal in writing this book is to give you a glimpse into their lives today, to reflect on the reasons for their longevity and vitality, and to learn from their experiences.

We have to wonder: what gave them the support, the spirit and the resilience to overcome challenges and barriers in their long lives? Was it an understanding parent or compassionate teacher? A good education? Growing up in a small town? Or was it simply old-fashioned luck—having good genes or the good fortune to be at the right place at the right time?

Women who are over seventy-five can change how we look at old age. Rather than viewing mature women as dull and static—sitting around watching television all day or waiting for the mail to arrive—many forward thinkers now see old age as a period of growth: a stage of *becoming*, not just being. This is an innovative way of looking at aging. This is not a denial of old age but a realization that the later years are a *developmental period*, just like adolescence or midlife. As you will see when you meet the women in this book, they are not only living their lives fully, just as they did when they were younger, but they are continuing to grow and develop as women.

Of course, this is not true for everyone, but for those women who continue to stay productive and involved in life throughout their eighties and nineties, these years can be rich and rewarding. Those are the women we can emulate as role models and those are the women featured in this book.

This project began out of professional curiosity. I had interviewed women from age fifty-five through seventy-five for my last book, *Coming Home to Yourself: Eighteen Wise Women Reflect on Their Journeys.* I wondered now, what about those over seventy-five? Who are these women? What keeps them going despite physical decline and losses in so many areas of their lives? Is it truly a joy or is it a burden to live into your eighties and nineties? I was also curious about how these older women balanced and blended the many aspects of their lives into a unified whole.

To explore these questions, I wanted to do an in-depth study of their experiences as older women. I was drawn to highly accomplished women: two had taught at the college level, one was a *New York Times* bestselling author, another a physician at a time when very few women enrolled in medical school. But when I interviewed Bea Klein, a homemaker from Las Cruces, something shifted for me. It brought back many memories of my mother, who was a smart woman and content to spend her days focusing on my father, my sister and me. Like Bea, my mother did not have a college education. Rather than having a career, she did a lot of volunteer work. In fact, she and Bea even volunteered at the same places: the hospital auxiliary and the synagogue. Their pride and joy were their husbands and children.

I wonder what my mother would have been like if she had survived past age seventy-one. Would she have also led a rich, full life like the women I interviewed had she lived into her eighties or nineties? What traits or characteristics ensure longevity not in years alone but in quality of life? My professional curiosity in this project now deepened to include a much more personal motivation to explore the answers to the questions I posed.

Did these women have better genes or did my mother not have the passion, resiliency or meaning in life that can lead to long years? Many women received satisfaction from their roles as homemakers, mothers and wives during the 1940s and '50s, but let's not forget the other women who stifled in those roles, who Betty Friedan touched when she spoke of "the problem that has no name."

Women who chose (or had little choice) to be homemakers deserve our respect as much as those who earned Ph.Ds. Our society does not value them equally, however, even in the twenty-first century. This is not the place for a discussion of the mommy wars except to note that some of the women who lived into their eighties and nineties who led

10

so-called ordinary, 1950s-housewife-type lives—like June Cleaver—must have had something in their earlier decades that prepared them for a fulfilling late age. It could be genes, experiences, relationships, or education. And the women who have led more "interesting," high-achieving lives also must have had earlier experiences that led them to the same place today.

It seems to me that it was not the graduate education or the career successes that led to their longevity, but other ingredients that they shared with the so-called ordinary women. Perhaps both had strong parents, challenging teachers, solid relationships, or an experience that they faced and overcame that built their long-lasting resilience. In other words, it might not be *the external events* of a woman's life but the internal, emotional, or psychological forces and influences that forge the resilience that provide the basis for a woman to live well for nine or ten decades.

The Face Of Aging Today

Everyone knows that baby boomers (those born between 1946 and 1964) are changing the face of aging, that they are transforming the way we regard the years between sixty and seventy, and how we view retirement. And they're transforming it in a noisy way; we all know they are there. They now number thirty-five million, about half of whom are women.

But baby boomers tell only part of the story. There is also an unsung group of individuals who are living longer and leading active, engaged lives: those over the age of seventy-five. According to the *National Jewish Population Study* (2011), they comprise nine percent of the Jewish population. That is almost 500,000 people and women form more than half of this older group. These women remain invisible in our youth-oriented culture; you do not usually read about them in the media, but they personally touch many of us. When I was looking for women in this age bracket to interview for this book, so many people said to me, "Oh, you must meet so-and-so. She is an amazing woman!"

These women are all around us and we can learn from their examples. Not only because they are amazing but also because younger generations need role models to show us how to live the years past age seventy-five. We desperately want and need advice and guidance. We want to know what it's really like to have outlived your best friends, to see a great grandchild struggle, to cope with an aging body.

And we want to know how they contend with the existential questions of aging. In her book *Composing a Further Life*, writer and cultural anthropologist Mary Catherine Bateson raises an essential question for older women to ponder: "How do I grow older and remain myself—or rather, how in growing older do I become more truly myself, and how is that expressed in what I do or say or contribute?"

These are important questions for us to reflect on as we age, because women have not lived this long in large numbers before. There is no template for these later years: That's the rub *and* the opportunity—for all of us.

The Secret To Longevity

Everyone wants to know the secret to a long life. Is it eating yogurt for years? A particular DNA? A study of long-lived Ashkenazi Jews has found that those who drank slightly more and exercised less than their average counterparts lived longer. But their longevity had nothing to do with their religion.

In central Italy, people believe their dietary habits hold the key to their longevity. No one in Campodimele takes short cuts. They bring down logs from nearby hills on horseback to fuel their wood-burning stoves, make their own olive oil and pasta, and harvest their own grain. Meals can take hours to prepare. Many Japanese, on the other hand, credit their diet of vegetables and tofu and other soy products as the reason they live so long.

Here in the United States, it's not diet but resilience that researchers are beginning to realize might hold the secret to living a long life. According to Al Siebert, Ph.D., founder of The Resiliency Center and author of *The Resiliency Advantage*, "Longevity research is showing that adults with psychological resiliency age more slowly, live longer, and enjoy better health. A strong inner spirit can carry an aging body a long ways."

A related study by British epidemiologist Michael Marmot, seen in his 2005 book, *The Status Syndrome: How Social Standing Affects Our Health and Longevity,* provided evidence that the people who age successfully do so because they have considerable control over their lives as well as strong social support. Taking control is an aspect of resilience: It is an active role rather than passively waiting on the sideline for something to happen. It is this sense of agency, of get-up-and-go, that serves people well in old age. And certainly, monetary security helps as well.

Numerous studies have shown the importance of social support throughout the life span. This holds true as we age. Last summer when I was at the Jersey shore, an acquaintance, who is in her early eighties, invited me to meet her bridge group. They were convening in her apartment the following evening. These nine Jewish women, between the ages of seventy-five and eight-five, have been playing bridge together for over fifty years. They were attractive and took care with their appearance. When I told them about the book, they were fascinated and full of questions. Then we went around the room and each woman spoke for a few minutes about her life.

They had all lived in the Atlantic City/Margate area for most of their lives. Many left to go to school and then returned. Most of their children followed the same pattern and have settled in the area. Every one there had experienced some kind of hardship: one woman had been homeless and lived out of her car for a while, several had lost children and husbands, a few had serious health issues.

"What helped you overcome adversity?" I asked when they had finished speaking. They all agreed: their small town roots and their long-standing friendships. The security of living "where everyone knows your name" and the support of good friends created a foundation that enabled them to rebound from whatever challenging situations they encountered during their long lives.

The Only Constant Is Change

The only thing that remains unchanged in our lives—no matter our age, religion, lifestyle, economics or culture—is change. Some changes are thrust upon us; others we welcome willingly. Both invite a deeper understanding of ourselves, if we're open to such reflection.

As we have seen in recent years, everything—from the climate to politics to electronics—is constantly in flux. We have so little control. We can only manage our responses: how we accept and adapt to shifts, whether we roll with the punches, or remain rigid and static can affect our lives in ways both beneficial and destructive.

From my research and writing about psychological topics and women's issues, I believe that the more adaptable we are, the longer we'll live. The more open to transitions and the more willing to try variations, the more likely we are to grow and expand. This attitude keeps us young and vibrant in mind and spirit, and better able to cope with the physical changes of aging. After years of research on resilience in children and adolescents, recent studies now point to resilience as a key factor in explaining who thrives among the oldest of the old.

Other research has shown that those women who experienced the most discontinuity and change *earlier* in life became most vital later, while those who clung to a single outdated role ended up frustrated and depressed. This means that women's continual engagement and letting go—of children, careers, and partners—prepared them well for the shifts of old age and could account for their greater flexibility and resilience later in life. Author Anna Quindlen had it right when she wrote, ".... women's lives have been about re-definition, over and over again, while men's lives are still often about maintaining the status quo."

The Blessing Of Good Luck

We talk of the importance of having resilience, of finding passions and meaning in life. But another factor can play an enormous role in how our later years turn out: luck. The fortunate ones are bestowed with good luck. Others work hard, do the right thing, and yet do not get what they deserve. Life is not fair.

Alice Ladas, who is ninety-two, commented on how her good fortune contributed to her longevity when I interviewed her. She said, "The fact is, I have been lucky. I have not had a major accident or major health problem. I have not been run over by a car. I was not at the twin towers when they fell." To some, that could make her an unsympathetic exception—rather than an exemplary person—because she has not struggled enough.

On the other hand, good luck alone might not be sufficient to create longevity. Sara/Hannah Rigler, whom you'll also meet in these pages, observed that there is another step that must follow luck for it to be truly utilized. In her book she wrote,

"Some would say I have been lucky and I have—but luck only impacts if you grab onto it and use it to help yourself and others. In an airplane the stewardess tells you in case of emergency to use the oxygen first, and then help the less able. I have spent my life following this admonition. I kept myself alive by resisting death when I left the line of the death march. I kept myself alive even when I fell into deep despair at the news that my mother and sister perished. I kept myself alive so that my family and my people would continue."

Indeed, she has seized her luck and used it to keep herself and future generations alive.

The Jewish Connection

The Jewish attitude toward aging differs from the general attitude prevalent in twenty-first century Western society. Jewish views are based on a unique respect for the wisdom that comes with age and a reverence for our own parents and the elderly in general. The Torah commands that we respect all elderly, believing that the challenges and experiences they have encountered throughout their lives bring wisdom. The Torah also considers old age a virtue and a blessing and often equates "old" (*zakein*) with "wise." Thus, a ripe old age is regarded as one of the greatest blessings we can experience.

Of course, we all endorse these beliefs in theory but they might not play out so consistently in real life. Older Jewish women still experience the ageism and sexism prevalent among all older women. The stereotype of the Jewish mother who is overprotective, nagging and guilt-producing remains alive and well. Clichés also abound for the *kvetch* (someone who is constantly complaining) and the demure, self-sacrificing widow.

These stereotypes are not far from the concept of crone, a stock character of an old woman in folklore and fairy tale. Sometimes she is portrayed as nasty or evil but often with magical powers. On the positive side, a crone can be viewed as an archetypal figure, a Wise Woman—not simply *any* older woman. In the last thirty years, many older women have begun connecting to the crone and her positive attributes: wisdom, kindness, and transformation. Identifying with this archetype affirms the knowledge, insights, and intuition that accompany aging.

The women in this book represent twelve different life experiences and twelve unique ways of aging with wisdom and vitality. I have chosen the number twelve because it is a significant one in Judaism. Twelve is considered one of the perfect numbers. Jacob had twelve sons, who were the ancestors of the twelve tribes of Israel. I hope the twelve women in this book will help replace some of the stereotypical figures with a more realistic view of older Jewish women.

About This Book

Although this book favors career women—at a time when it was not easy or automatic to go to college—the main criteria for selecting and profiling these women is their resilience and vibrancy in "older age," regardless of their educational or career achievements.

To find women who met these qualifications, I began by sending an email to a select group of friends, acquaintances, and colleagues. I sifted through their recommendations and when I found someone who seemed well suited, I asked her to fill out a short survey so I could obtain some background information. The survey also asked some deeper questions, including: What were three major changes or transformations that occurred during your life and how did you respond to them? How did your earlier life prepare you for life as an older woman? How did your connection to Judaism impact on your life?

Their answers to these questions helped me decide whether the woman had the insight and thoughtfulness this project required. Once I selected a woman, I interviewed her for several hours (often broken up into small segments), sometimes on the phone and sometimes in person, depending on where she lived.

With the resilience research in mind, I focused on how they have adapted to change over the years and in their current life. I explored whether and how their response has shifted as they have aged, how the understanding they have gained has contributed to their longevity, and how they cope today with the transitions and losses that aging brings. I also delved into the ramifications of those changes on their lives today by exploring how these women see their old age as a product and reflection of the choices and adaptations they made earlier in their lives.

All the women in the book were born Jewish and are grandmothers. Most continue to practice Judaism today and strive for a spiritual life in some form. They range from observant to cultural Jews. Some have rejected organized religion but have incorporated the principles of Judaism into their lives and are living according to those standards. Others are still actively involved in synagogue life. One finds meaning in Jewish meditation; another has left the fold altogether.

Each woman has her own chapter. It begins with her photo as a way to combat the invisibility that so many older women feel. You can visualize her as you read her chapter and realize that yes, this is what ninety looks like. The chapter combines the narrative of her life with her thoughts and reflections about her experiences, excerpted from our interviews. Direct quotes from the interviewees are in italics. Each woman had an opportunity to read her chapter before it went to press so that she could check the facts.

"The Privilege Of Aging"

While many of us lament growing older and wish we were younger, the fact is, it is a privilege to age—especially when you consider the alternative. Coping with an aging body, losing friends and family, becoming ill: these take their toll. We all have unique ways of responding to these shifts based on who we are, what our earlier life has been like, and how we feel about ourselves today.

Actress Laura Linney coined the phrase "the privilege of aging" in a July 28, 2010 article in *The New York Times*. She talked about aging, and about how she was mystified and frustrated with so many people's rebellion against aging. She conceded that "sagging skin, waning energy and creaky joints are not fun," but said that the early deaths of beloved friends had opened her eyes to the fact that growing old is the greatest of blessings. "A lot of people do not get that privilege," she said. "And there is an extreme disrespect toward that that is cuckoo." Whenever she realizes that she is about to complain about aging, she imagines one of her friends who has died taking her by the shoulders and shaking her and saying: "Snap out of it!"

I hope that the twelve women in this book will inspire you and remind you that aging is indeed a privilege. Each of the women represents a different way of aging with grace, consciousness, wisdom and gratitude. Their willingness to share their life journey, including their triumphs over tragedy, is indeed a gift. On a personal note, I have accepted the fact that my mother was unable to give me the legacy of long years, and that I will never know why she died so young. But I realize now that she gave me a model of how to be a caring mother and grandmother, a supportive wife, and a good friend.

The women in this book also leave their legacies in many forms. Read about them and then select the women's journeys that resonate with you. Make these women your role models so that the way *you* live your later years can be a legacy, and a blessing for your family and friends.

Paula Amar Schwartz, 79
Centered in the Midst of Change

IT IS A PERFECT NEW MEXICO FALL day: a brilliant blue sky, leaves turning shades of red and yellow, a nip in the air. Guitar music plays softly as we enter the sanctuary and take a seat in the circle of chairs set up in a corner. After a brief introduction, we begin with a guided meditation focused on our breath. Hebrew chants follow and then we do a meditation using Hebrew letters as mantra. Next, we chant the *Shema* (the central prayer of Judaism) slowly, one breath to each word. Through conscious breathing, chanting, and reflecting, we turn inward and grow calm and centered.

This is Jewish meditation. It is at the center of Paula Amar Schwartz's life—and centers her life. She has practiced meditation for fifty years and has taught for over twenty. It has been part of her healing from a divorce, the death of another husband, and the loss of a son. It aids her in coping with Parkinson's disease. It has made her more receptive and resilient, opened her to poetry, and allowed her creativity to flourish. In short, Jewish meditation has transformed her life.

As a yogi who is Jewish, I was fascinated by the concept of meditation with a Jewish focus, so when an acquaintance told me that she has been in a Jewish meditation group with Paula for three years and saw up close how Paula had overcome challenging experiences with the aid of meditation, I was eager to meet this resilient woman.

Another thing intrigued me about Paula: She leaves Albuquerque for the summer and goes to Ocean City, New Jersey. I also leave Santa Fe and go to the Jersey shore for part of the summer. Not many people from the Southwest do this so I was curious about what else she and I might share.

Last summer, I learned more about what we have in common when I interviewed her one hot July morning at her beach house at the southern most tip of Ocean City. A cup of herbal tea and a sticky bun were waiting for me when I arrived. We sat at a big rectangular wooden table in her great room, overlooking the dunes, a deep beach, and the waves lapping the shore. Her husband Mel came in and out of the room, reminding her that we had to finish up by noon so they could go to a Tai Chi class together.

As cool ocean breezes wafted in, Paula shared the journey of her life. She grew up in Pittsburgh, the only child of a park supervisor and a nurse. Her grandparents, who had emigrated from Hungary, lived with them. Her grandfather worked as a furrier and played the flute and violin. Paula remembers the air raid drills during World War II; from the time she was five until she was about eleven, they would all take refuge in the basement.

My grandfather would play the flute and Uncle Jack would play a spinet piano. On the other side of the room we had a washing machine and clothes hanging on the line. I loved to dance, so I would dance to the music. Often times, it was like a party. It never occurred to me to be afraid.

Paula grew up in a secular household but her parents insisted she go to Sunday school. When she was sixteen, her rabbi gave her and the other students a piece of paper with their Confirmation reading on it. She read hers and felt it did not sound like her, so she told him, "I can't read this. I'll write something that sounds like me that you'll be proud of." He replied, "You'll read what I wrote because your parents will be very disappointed if you're not confirmed."

I thought about it, read what he wrote, and was confirmed in order not to disappoint my parents. But I left the synagogue and did not return for twenty plus years. He lost me to Judaism, though I credit him for teaching me scholarship. He was a great scholar, a fine historian and literary critic. I loved hearing his sermons. In addition, he gave me a great blessing: he provided me an opportunity to wander and explore spirituality. I roamed through Quakers, Unitarians, Buddhists and Hindus. I had a revelation while I was sitting in a Buddhist setting, chanting in Sanskrit. I asked myself: "Why am I sitting here chanting in a language I do not understand? Maybe it's time to go home and learn Hebrew."

Her sons were eight and four at the time; she was newly divorced. She joined a synagogue and began to study Hebrew. Several years later, she met Rabbi Zalman Schachter-Shalomi, who her husband Henri knew as a colleague at Temple University. Reb Zalman's Hasidic Judaism was evolving into an innovative, spiritually-informed Judaism that became the Jewish Renewal Movement. She was pleased to be able to study with him.

During those years when she left Judaism, her life had unfolded. She went to Antioch College where she started as a dance major, then realized she could not make a living dancing so graduated with a joint major in psychology and sociology. She met her first husband in New York City on one of her coop jobs as a social worker at Harlem House on the Upper East side. They married three months after they met at a socialist meeting, then returned to Antioch so that she could complete her last year and graduate. He enrolled at the University of New Mexico so they moved to Albuquerque. She started grad school and he became a theatre major. They stayed there for seven years while her husband dropped in and out of school; then they moved to the Philadelphia area.

Paula worked for the Devereux Schools for children with autism disorders and other special needs until she learned that the Medical College of Pennsylvania was starting an experimental program leading to a Ph.D. in health psychology. She enrolled and was just about ready to finish her dissertation when her marriage collapsed. She was fed up with her husband's instability and infidelities and finally realized that she could not change him, even though she had tried for years. When she told her husband she was through, he replied, "You cannot leave me. How will you support yourself? You're still in school." As she walked out the door, she retorted, "Watch me."

I was in the process of divorce, but needed to get a loan so I could finish my dissertation. I'll never forget the day I walked into the local bank. "I would like to apply for a loan," I said to the loan officer. "We do not give loans to women," he replied. It was 1970, the women's movement had begun, and women were in the news with legal precedents and challenges. "Oh, yes," I said, "I think you would best go upstairs and tell your CEO and your bank lawyer that you just said you do not give loans to women. I'm going to court to sue you."

He left the room and went up the marble staircase, leaving me to sit and wait. I did not know if I had just burnt my bridge to freedom or would find another way. Forty- five minutes later, three men in three-piece suits came down the marble staircase, and I knew I had won my battle. Yes, I had to document my life. Yes, I had to sign off on the unpaid loan my husband had taken and not repaid. Yes, I had to agree to bring in my divorce papers as soon as they were filed. But I got my loan. That was a turning point.

Paula finished her doctorate and repaid her loan. A medical school hired her to become director of its biofeedback program. Biofeedback is a process of gaining greater awareness of physiological functions, initially using instruments that provide information on the activity of those systems, with a goal of being able to manipulate them at will. She hired a staff and began studies in how meditation techniques can alter physiology. She learned that we all have the capacity to change our bodies and that we can normalize things that have gone out of control and bring them back into a state of equilibrium. While studying Buddhist meditation, she became a regular meditator herself.

Meditation has influenced my life enormously. The years that I have been meditating have opened my eyes and made me aware of the beauty around me. Becoming more receptive is a way of being resilient. It's such an opening process. It's a way of awakening that sense of wonder.

The meditation process has been part of my healing when I have had to transcend difficulties. To be able to go inside, quiet myself, and then move forward is what meditation has done for me. It does not necessarily speed up the healing process, but it makes it more tolerable. Healing takes time and is different for everyone. I found that being able to be quiet and turn inward—because you're full of thoughts of the person you lost—allows you to go beyond that, so everything does not begin and end with what I'm struggling with—anger, grief, whatever. You need to go into it and not avoid it. Meditation helps you do that.

Even when grief is fresh, meditation has worked for me. It's not dwelling on what's lost but going through it into something that's bigger than that. It's based on the whole idea of what came before and after this life. Without sounding too far out, I would suggest that the meditation process has opened me to the possibility that there's something beyond this lifetime and that helps a lot. It makes me less

24

important. It makes the loss of a loved one every bit as real but not the end of everything, because we might very well meet again.

Two years after her divorce, she married Henri Amar, a theoretical physicist. They blended their families in Ambler, Pennsylvania and started a whole new life. This time she thought it would be forever, but he developed lung cancer and died eight years later. When he was diagnosed and began treatment, she needed to cut back her hours so she could be there for him and her sons.

When I told my department chair that I needed to reduce my work to half time and be home half time, I expected him to understand. He looked at me and said, "But, Paula, we need someone who can teach, and run the clinic, and do the consulting. We need you to do your job." I did not comprehend. "I cannot do it all," I said. "I need to be home part time, and work around what's happening." "Well, now, my girl," he said, "buck up, you're not the only person to have family problems. You would not quit a tenured track position, my dear, would you?" "Yes, I would," I said. "You'll have my resignation in the morning."

She left, not knowing what she would do, but fully aware of what had to be done. She packed up her office in two weeks and turned the small cottage next door to their house into Ambler Psychological Services. Within six weeks of opening her new practice, she had more patients than she could handle.

In the year after her second husband's death, tennis became her elixir, creating an interesting balance: venting her anger and sorrow through tennis and going inward for healing and serenity during meditation.

Tennis sustained me, nourished me, and allowed me a way to vent my anger, sorrow, emptiness, and loss without social consequences. It also allowed me to socialize without talking about or facing the emotions I so carefully interred deeply inside. I played with friends, in tournaments, in doubles, singles, and round robins.

After the first month, I went back to work: tending patients, teaching classes, offering seminars, publishing papers— burying myself so that I could come home at night, care for my son, our house, the garden, the trappings of life. Everyone thought I was handling it all so well, but I was only partly there. The other part sat in the cemetery carrying on a conversation with my dear one, who had the audacity to leave me behind. "How dare you go away and leave me to deal with this mess!" I sat there and screamed at him. I yelled at God as well.

Time—that rubber band of relativity, which Henri had worked so hard to understand—had expanded. It stretched an hour into a day, a day into a year, a year into an infinity of mindless time. But on the tennis court, time contracted. An hour and a half of group time passed in a moment; a peaceful, focused, companionable moment.

On the tennis court she met her third husband Mel Schwartz, whom she has been with for thirty years. Overall, they have been good years except for the tragedy of losing her son Aaron at age thirty-one. A medical student with Crohn's disease, he died of a sudden crashing of the red blood cell system, a rare side effect of one of his medications. Coping with his death was far harder than dealing with her husband's.

The death of a child is so out of the natural order of things. There is a whole section in my poetry book on when the 'sun' is gone. I do not know how I got through it. Meditation certainly helped and I guess the rest of life just pulled me in. There was too much else that was going on that took priority and attention. I just kept on living even though I was not all there. A part of me had drowned. I was under water with seaweed coming out of my ears. One day during the summer of Aaron's death I was walking along the beach and realized I put on a really good show. Everyone thought I was fine but I was not. I called my doctor and asked for the best grief therapist I could find. That's when I learned those techniques of talking to those who are gone so I could say goodbye. That made a huge difference.

Twenty years ago Paula and Mel moved from Philadelphia to Albuquerque and have built a full life there. Paula plays tennis, skis, swims, and hikes. She is active in community organizations, writes poetry, and teaches meditation and other subjects. She is close to her son Adam, an environmental attorney, who lives northwest of Philadelphia with his wife and two children. She maintains the house at the beach to bring together Adam's family with Henri and Mel's children, and an array of grandchildren.

In 2008 when she was about to celebrate her seventy-fifth birthday, she decided that rather than throwing a big party, she preferred to commemorate the event by publishing her first book of poetry. She is very proud of *Beyond Time and Space* and plans to publish a second book of poetry for her eightieth birthday.

Like many of the women I interviewed, Paula does not feel her age. She feels more like she is between fifty and sixty years old. She knows she feels older than forty but because she has Parkinson's disease, she also knows what it's like to feel "old." Some days parts of her body tighten up and she has to be careful to rest. Besides taking medication, she works with an acupuncturist and an energy healer. She also uses meditation to control the Parkinson's. She drops into her body when it starts to tremble, lets it release, and then the trembling quiets.

Clearly, meditation has served her well. But I wondered, whether she felt that anything else has contributed to her resilience.

Growing up during the war years and the resourcefulness and resilience of my parents, whose life was difficult, but I never felt that it was. I regret that my parents died before I could say that I appreciate them and what they did. They were role models for me. They did not complain; they were very matter of fact. I remember the night the telegram came from Lily, the sole survivor of our family in Hungary, telling us that her parents and aunts and uncles had all perished in the Holocaust. My parents were frustrated but they did not dwell on it. They called Uncle Jack, who served as family lawyer, asked him to reach out to her and offer to help, and then went back to cutting the vegetables and doing the preserving and canning. That's the way it was. I remember noticing that my dad's shoe had a hole in the bottom with cardboard filling the hole. It never occurred to me that he could not afford to replace the shoes. I thought everyone's shoes had cardboard in them.

During the difficult years when I was finishing my doctorate and money was short, it never occurred to me to complain about it. I just did what needed to be done. I learned how to shop and feed my boys on ten dollars a week; I made hotdog stew, which they loved. When I have abundance, it's good but if it were not there, I know I would be okay. Because I have survived with limited resources, I do not take anything for granted. I have been on the other side and when I encounter people going through a rough time, I do not judge them because I know that there but for the grace of God, go I.

But I have to go back to meditation: It allows me to tune in to something that's larger than myself and that gives me a sense of humility. It helps me realize that everything that happens is not of my doing. But I'm open to whatever happens. If we think we're directing life, we're mistaken. But I have to stress: I do not look at myself as an unusual individual. I'm someone who has learned these skills. They are tools that anyone can learn.

Another tool that has been helpful to her is cultivating gratitude, something that she would encourage younger women to explore.

28

Look around you. See the children. See the mountains. See the ocean. Be aware of the apples on the tree. Notice the sound of the wind in the aspen leaves. Awareness of the gifts of the world is the first step toward gratitude.

Traditional Judaism is actually a practice of awareness; there is a blessing for seeing the first fruit on the tree, for seeing a rainbow, and for meeting a scholar or leader. There is a blessing for everything, and when there is not a blessing, there is the Shecheyanu, which praises the Eternal One for keeping us alive, sustaining us, and allowing us to reach this moment of awareness. Once the awareness emerges, gratitude follows.

I wondered what other advice she has for younger women, and she said:

Cultivate an array of things that gives you pleasure and joy. Have them be different: have something that's physical: hiking, swimming, or tennis. Get good at it, cultivate it, and get those memories into your body system so it remembers it when you're older and it's harder. Find something like painting or music. Whatever you love to do, keep doing it and stay current in your field, especially when you retire. Read all the new research. Learn new skills. I thanked my class for making me learn Power Point. I have had to teach myself a whole new set of abilities. The same thing with friendships: cultivate them and appreciate them.

Even though many of the women in this book told me they feel younger than their chronological age, they also experienced a point when they felt "old." Paula has not yet reached that point but she has given it much thought.

I know I'll have that day when my body will not do what I want it to do. Then I start thinking…That's fine as long as I still have my sphincters and my mind. If those go, it's time for me to check out. I have done the paper work for informed consent; my kids are all informed. If my body will do enough of the things I need it to do, I'm fine. I came to that some time ago when I was with a dying friend.

I have been aware for some time that there is a transition point, a way in which our spirit transcends the passing of the body. I do believe there is a thin veil between the two worlds. I'm concerned about living to an old age and being incapacitated, but I'm not afraid of dying.

As someone who has faced loss and rebounded from it many times during her almost eight decades, Paula Amar Schwartz often reflects on the meaning of life in her writing and in her meditation. The following excerpt from an essay she wrote sums up the philosophy that has served her so well.

Life IS a journey, often more like an exploration into unknown territory. Sometimes, in a dream like way, what appeared to be new territory has been a circle back to a familiar place, and other times, what appeared known and familiar, becomes new and fresh…Every time I think I know where my life is going, some change takes place and the path goes in some unexpected direction. This has stopped surprising me. I am increasingly comfortable waiting to see what will be around the next switchback. Like the adventure of hiking a trail, I am not so much surprised by the new view of a river far below, or the flash of an eagle's wing, or the puma sunning himself in a clearing, as I am in awe of each chance moment.

30

Ruth Leebron, 89
A Peripatetic Life

W HEN RUTH LEEBRON GREW UP IN THE small town of Carnegie, Oklahoma (population two thousand), she knew it marked a temporary stop on her lifelong journey. Her father always encouraged her to reach for a better life: a life filled with education, culture and travel. "This is not your life," he would often remind her. "You'll leave here and settle elsewhere."

Not only did she leave Carnegie, but she moved thirty-two times during her life. Some of the moves were by choice, but most were by circumstance. In both cases, she adapted to new and foreign surroundings and cultures with a buoyant, can-do spirit. That spirit continues to serve her well as an older woman.

One of the women featured in my last book, who lives in Oklahoma City, suggested I contact Ruth for this book. She told me, "Ruth is widowed, a retired university professor, extremely beautiful. She still travels extensively and looks like she is fifty." That combination of traits sounded intriguing to me.

In our telephone conversations, Ruth told me that her parents were born in Poland and settled in Carnegie, ninety miles southwest of Oklahoma City, because they had family there. Her father went into the department store business with his relatives. The town was a farming community, and most of the residents were not educated beyond high school. Ruth's family was the only Jewish one in town, which led to some problems. When all her friends were invited to a party and Ruth was not, a friend would take her aside and whisper to her, "You were not invited because you're Jewish." That made her feel like an outsider but did not keep her from making friends. Her brother, almost two years older, experienced antisemitism in a more blatant way. He often came home from grade school with a black eye: another day when the kids called him a "dirty Jew."

Their mother was strict with them. They had to be on their best behavior because they were the only Jewish kids in town, and she did not want anyone pointing a finger at them. On the other hand, she held liberal views. When Ruth was in sixth grade, she allowed her to go to the Christian Sunday School with her friends. Each week, her mother would remind her, "Learn what you can, but remember that we do not believe that Jesus is the Son of God."

Ruth's parents belonged to a synagogue in Oklahoma City. They drove there on a two-lane, unpaved road for the High Holidays; they also went in each Sunday to buy for the store and then stayed for dinner and a movie. When the symphony started in 1936, they bought season tickets. They thought nothing of arriving home at 2 a.m., sated from their cultural fix.

Like many Jewish merchants worldwide, they decorated the store for Christmas, but lit Chanukah candles at home. They did not observe *Shabbat* (the Sabbath), however, because they both worked in the store on Friday nights, but they did have a Passover Seder at home each year.

I was very conscious of my Jewishness because I was an outsider and because my life was so restricted. I felt under wraps in Carnegie. I knew I would be freer if I had Jewish friends, people my mother approved of. There were certain things I could not do, like going to a dance. That's why I was so anxious to be in a Jewish community. As a teenager, my folks would drive me any place in Oklahoma to be with other Jewish children. They made every effort to keep me happy being Jewish.

At the University of Oklahoma Ruth created a Jewish community for herself and dated Jewish boys for the first time. She met her first husband (yes, he was Jewish) and the father of her two daughters there. After they married, he joined the army and became an officer; she went to work as an accountant—at a time when most women became nurses, teachers and secretaries.

I loved math but the only thing you could do with math is teach. I wanted to go to engineering school, but my father did not want me to because I would be the only woman. So I went into Business Administration and got a degree in accounting with a minor in Finance. Then I applied to the largest private firm in Oklahoma City for a job and was the first woman they hired. This was 1945. After I sat in the office doing grunt work for awhile, I said, "I would like to go on an audit." My boss said, "My clients would think I would lost my mind if I sent a woman." But they found me a business to audit where no one was in the office.

Ruth did not work while she raised her two daughters. For twenty-two years she followed her husband from army post to army post: Baltimore, Washington, D.C., Leavenworth, Kansas, and Tokyo, Japan were among their stops. She had a fatalistic attitude about all the upheavals for their family.

This is the life of an army wife. You just do it. The army packs you and moves you at no expense to you. But it's terribly uprooting, especially for the kids. They had a hard time with it. My oldest will tell you that she had a miserable childhood: every time she made a friend she had to leave. But it did not hurt her any: she was the first military child to be president of the student council in her high school. She was popular then and she is successful in business now.

My mother was displaced from Poland to Carnegie and she complained miserably about it. I felt at least I had my family. I got to the point where it was sort of fun. Coming from Carnegie, I never felt settled there; my folks were always going to Oklahoma City. I was a fish out of water. In the army, everyone is different, so it was not as bad as I thought it could be. I can hit the road running and make friends. You're all in the same boat so you make friends.

Whenever they traveled to a new place, one of their biggest challenges was to find other Jewish families. Ruth wanted her daughters to feel a sense of their Jewish identity, but in most places, few other Jewish officers or synagogues existed. If there were a temple nearby, they would join one. If there were a community Passover Seder, they would attend. In Germany, they drove one hundred kilometers to go to services.

Once the girls left home, with her husband stationed in Korea, Ruth went back to school and received an MBA and a CPA. She taught accounting at Oklahoma City University for thirty-five years. The last seventeen years of her career she held the position of Dean of International Studies and ran the Master's of Business Administration program in the Pacific Rim. She made twenty-eight trips to the Far East: China, Singapore, Taiwan, and Kuala Lumpur, among other places.

All that moving around as an army wife taught me to travel to strange places and do what I had to do. When I traveled to the Pacific Rim, I enjoyed every minute of it—the journey itself and working with the students. The Asian students were so anxious to learn, it made teaching a pleasure.

Following thirty-two years of marriage, her husband left her for a younger woman. She was crushed, but with her daughters' support, she put the marriage in perspective. After the divorce, she married husband #2, a colon-rectal surgeon whom she met on the tennis court, who died two years later of colon cancer. Seven years after his death, she married a popular retired reform rabbi from Oklahoma City, who was actually the rabbi of the synagogue to which she belonged and who had officiated at her two daughters' weddings. Ruth and Joe were married for fourteen years, until his death in 2006.

Had he not been a rabbi I would not have married again, but you cannot shack up with the rabbi! It was so easy being married to him. It was just fun being with him. Everyone loved him. In fact, my standing in the community improved when I was married to him!

Today, Ruth remains active in several organizations. She is vice president of the Jewish Federation, belongs to the Executive Service Corps, an organization of retired people who advise nonprofits in trouble, and served on the boards of Goodwill, Children's Convalescent Home, and the YWCA. She goes to exercise class three days a week, has three bridge games a week, and belongs to two book clubs.

Ruth has always exercised. She started playing tennis in her thirties and played into her seventies when she experienced some knee problems and had to quit. Other than taking radioactive iodine for her thyroid and blood pressure medication, she is in good health. She has lived longer than anyone in her family. It's possible that her extensive travels have made her so adaptable and resilient, but also her childhood as an isolated Jewish kid in the boondocks of Oklahoma prepared her for later life.

Time is different for me now. I'm traveling a lot. The reason is because I'm healthy and I'm getting older, and if I don't do it now, I might not be able to in the future. I can't put off anything. Time will end for me. You feel your mortality much stronger as you age. Everyday that I get up and feel well, I want to do something. If I don't do the things I want to do now, when will I?

I'm traveling to places I would not have dreamed of going. I'm going through the Panama Canal in December; I went around the horn of South America and to Argentina to meet relatives. Time is of the essence: I'm not going to jump out of an airplane but there is the sense that time is passing.

The hardest part about being my age is getting around although I'm still pretty adaptive. I'm still driving. My eyesight is good. I still walk on my own two feet and can go up and down steps. I really do not have problems getting around, which is unusual for my age. Actually, I do not feel my age. People tell me I don't look it. They say you're as old as you feel. Well, I feel like I'm in my sixties. People have accused me of acting like it too! Being active, I don't realize how old I am. I still have some spring in my step and I'm in pretty good shape.

The hard thing is that I have lost a lot of close friends; I went to two funerals just last week. That's why I have younger friends: Most women my age are gone, so I keep getting younger friends. Today most of my friends are ten to fifteen years younger. That keeps me younger, too.

Seeing Ruth's photo and hearing of her active, healthy life, many younger women would like to emulate her. I asked her what we younger women can do *now* to prepare for our later years.

Keep moving. Don't think you cannot do something until you try it. Don't give in to "I don't feel like that." A positive attitude is the best thing. There is no such thing as "I cannot do it." Try it. Find a way to get it accomplished. There is nothing that you cannot try. Of course, it's easier to stay home than go out. But if you stay home, then you get old. Your life stops moving. Get out among them. Sometimes it takes a lot of effort. The alternative is to let yourself get into a rut. Always try something new. You might like it.

I make myself keep moving and I have always had a good time doing it. I do have a full life. All my life I have been afraid of being bored so I always plan things so I won't be bored. I must have been bored as a child though I remember even then always having a project: cutting out paper dolls, making clothes for my dolls. I'm still that way. I cannot watch television unless I have a book on my lap so I can read during the commercials. I can drive myself crazy!

Some days I don't feel like getting out of bed but I do it anyhow. Usually this happens when I don't want to face something. The last few months I have had a little more down time than usual. I'm not sure why, but I have been able to take afternoon naps, which is unusual for me.

For the last twelve years, Ruth has lived in a house in a gated community containing eighty-two cottages for people aged fifty-five and older. Now, at age eighty-eight, she is contemplating a move from Oklahoma City to New York City, a transition that would feel colossal for most women her age. Both of her daughters live there and she feels this would be a good time to move because she is still healthy. When she reaches a point when she needs more help, her daughters will be nearby and can drop in.

I grew up being in New York a lot—my mother and I visited my aunt every summer— so moving there is no big deal. It's something that I have done forever—even before my girls moved there.

Everything in life is an experience that helps you meet challenges in later life. My family loved to travel so they taught me to travel and adapt. My travels as an army wife led me into my travels in my professional life. Now in my old age, I travel for pleasure many times a year, mostly to New York City to visit my daughters and their families. I grew up with a travel bug and I have not outgrown it yet.

Nona Chern, 91
A Voice for Justice

MANY PEOPLE SAY THEY BELIEVE IN JUSTICE but would not inconvenience themselves to prove it. Not Nona Chern. Throughout her long life, she has stood for justice and taken that extra step to make her voice heard, even though it was an unpopular stance and in one case, cost her a job.

A Professor Emerita and an award-winning teacher, Nona is an organizer, a go-getter and a force to be reckoned with at age ninety-one. Besides exercising, reading, belonging to a drama club and recently accepting the vice presidency of her synagogue, Nona helps her contemporaries write their ethical wills. She runs a luncheon once a month for one hundred "old ladies," The Prime Time Group, and recently delivered such a moving, personal *D'Var Torah* (a talk about a topic related to the weekly Torah portion, usually carrying a life lesson) at Friday night services that applause rocked the sanctuary. This year she also organized a Passover Seder at her retirement community for its eight Jewish residents; twenty-one non-Jews also attended.

A friend who's been in a Torah study group with Nona for eight years introduced me to her. She said, "Nona is bright, loves to talk, and is quite a character. Nothing seems to keep her down. Even when she has had medical issues, she keeps right on going." That sounded like a woman I would like to meet.

In our first phone interview, Nona told me that she spent the first ten years of her life in Atlantic City, New Jersey. At age eleven, in the midst of the depression, she and her parents moved to a Catholic working class neighborhood in West Philadelphia. Bankruptcy devastated the family; they lost everything. Her father hoped the change of location would offer him a fresh start. He tried selling liquor for a while; then his brother-in-law convinced him to open a restaurant with him. Even though he knew nothing about fish, Larchy's Oyster House became very successful—so successful that Nona would be able go to college later.

As a typical young girl, Nona was oblivious to her family's financial situation. She only knew that she grew up feeling loved by her large extended family. She was closer to her father, who treated her like the son he never had. They attended baseball and football games together and he even took her to the racetrack, and to boxing and wrestling matches, which she loved. Her parents were also big theatergoers and took her out of school anytime a musical came to town. This engendered her lifelong love of the theater.

One of Nona's most vivid childhood memories occurred during the first weeks at her new school. The experience left an indelible mark and set the beginning of her pattern of breaking boundaries.

I walk into the new school cold and only one person said to me, "I can walk you to class." She was Dorothy Washington, a black girl. She walked with me for two weeks and we became friends. One day a white girl comes up and says, "If you want to stay out of trouble, drop Dorothy." I did not see color here. I saw a girl who was being helpful. No one else was helping me. I thought to myself, "Who do you think you are?" I talked to Dorothy about it. She said, "My friends are saying the same thing to me. Maybe we should not talk to each other. It would be better for both of us." That hurt me so much. I had to accept something that I did not want to do or believe in.

Nona let her friendship with Dorothy go, but that early experience kindled her interest in justice. During her first job interview as a teacher, the interviewer asked, "As a Jewish person working for this school district, would you stay home on the Jewish holiday?" (In 1943 employers could ask such questions.) She replied that it depended on which holiday it was, but if it were the most important holiday of the year, yes, she would stay home. Then Nona turned the tables and asked the interviewer: "If you worked for a Jewish man and he asked you to work on Christmas day, what would you do?" The interviewer's jaw dropped.

I did not have to say that but I felt there was an injustice there. Needless to say, I did not get the job, but that experience put me on my way to asserting myself. I stood up for myself and for an injustice. I have to say that was a defining moment.

Nona met her husband David at the end of World War II. He had just come back from the Pacific as a Chief Petty Officer in the Navy and was on thirty-day leave. They married as soon as the war ended and he went into the insurance business. Looking back on their marriage, she remembers his unswerving devotion to her and their two children. He even took care of the children for two summers when she went to the University of Chicago for a special program, something most men did not do in those days.

Nona worked as a classroom teacher and a Reading Supervisor and Director in several Philadelphia area schools over the course of twenty-some years while she and her husband raised their son and daughter. When her son was in first grade, they helped start a reform congregation on Philadelphia's Main Line, which has become a congregation of eleven hundred families. This is where she attends her Torah study group. Today she considers her grown children and grandchildren dear friends. They have always been a close family and warmly welcomed their children's spouses into the fold when they married.

Certain incidents stand out in her long teaching career. When she was teaching sixth grade at a school in Southwest Philadelphia, a little girl in her class stood up and said, "They ought to send all the niggers back where they came from." Most of the children agreed with her, but Nona refused to let that comment pass.

I answered by saying, in that case, the Indians would be happy if all the white people went back where they belonged, too. I did not sleep that night, and began to wonder how I could change their intolerance. I went to the principal the next morning and told him about the incident, and what I would like to do. He gave me permission, with the understanding that he would like to stop in class from time to time. I packed up all their social studies and reading books and devised a plan to teach these courses through discussion, reading about immigrants, inviting foreign students to class, tracing their own family backgrounds and having relatives come in to talk to them. This was the first

41

course in tolerance taught in Philadelphia, and it was 1946. At the end of the year, the youngster who started it all told me the remark she made was dumb.

Five years after receiving a Master's in Education in Reading, Nona became an Assistant Professor of Elementary Education at West Chester University. They hired her without a doctorate and then promoted her to Associate Professor. She won an award as one of the top twenty-five teachers in the state. In 1982 she received her doctorate in Curriculum Theory and Instruction. When she applied to become a full professor, however, she ran into a major roadblock.

Three other women and I applied for full professorships. We were all turned down because we were women. We went to the Pennsylvania Human Relations Commission and filed a class action sex discrimination suit. It took five years but we won! We were all promoted to full professors. It was a landmark case and made all the newspapers.

During the last ten years of her teaching career, Nona dealt with a challenge of another sort. Her husband accidentally fell asleep in the sauna; the excessive and intensive heat caused him to lose most of his memory. He had to give up his business and could never work or drive again. He was sixty-two at the time. She became his caregiver and also took responsibility for the house, the finances, and everything else he did. At the time, she was working on her dissertation, which "saved" her life by giving her a diversion. He died around the same time that she retired from teaching, near her seventieth birthday. That was a difficult period for her but it did not keep her down.

You do what you have to do. It's not survival; it's a question of going on. I do not look back. I'm not sorry for anything I did. That's a waste of time. And I cannot worry about the future. I live in the present: I have good relationships with my children and grandchildren, and my two great grandchildren. They end each phone conversation with "I love you." My grandson even said he owed part of his success to me.

After her husband's death, Nona lived in a condo by herself until she moved into a retirement community in January 2012. Even there, at age ninety, she continues to stand up for injustices she observes. She noticed that when she moved into the facility everyone was very friendly. On her first night, they (an amorphous group that "greets" newcomers) invited her to join them for dinner but then she never saw them again; they only wanted to eat with their established friends. They did not have any intention of upsetting the status quo. Nona faced a wall of "This is my seat" and "We always sit together." She observed that all the new women, particularly the single ones, faced the same pattern. She is trying to change that—by inviting newcomers to dinner more than once and being more welcoming to people who move in. The administration supports her in this.

Moving into a retirement community from living independently was a big change. "There are a lot of old people here," Nona told her granddaughter, who replied, "Well, you're old too." They had a laugh over that. Actually, it was not until ten years ago that Nona felt she was aging.

I never thought of myself as old. I was just getting older. Women my age do not consider themselves old unless they're decrepit. I have found that the older I got, the more I looked back at my so-called salad days. Now I understand that introspection is an important part of aging. Once I admitted to myself that physically I could not dance all night, I realized that I still had a very active brain and the energy to use what I did have. I was eighty-one when this happened, and I only began to think along these lines because I was going to become a great grandmother. But I did feel a difference at that age, though it was gradual.

It takes me longer to do things. It can take me a half an hour to change the sheets on my queen-size bed. I do not have the stamina I had before. But it doesn't stop me. I take each step as it comes and deal with what I can. What I cannot, I cannot. I have a disability too. Neuropathy upsets my balance and walking without support for any length of time is very difficult. I can walk easily on the treadmill—and do—because I can hold on to the rails.

We all deal with forgetfulness of varying degrees and it's difficult to see friends becoming senile. One of the things that keeps me sharp is doing The New York Times *cross word puzzles and double crostics. I'm a word person. I have been with the same people in my* Torah *study for fourteen years. We're growing old together.*

I do have a positive attitude. If I were going to be anything else, I would be miserable. I could not live that way. There are times I'm not happy. I cannot do anything about some things, but I do not want to make myself depressed. Events can make you sad, but there is nothing you can do about certain things—my husband getting ill, my grandson dying of leukemia at twenty-four. You have to deal with the hand you're given.

Yes, you have to try to accept the hand you're given, but you can help influence the hand of those you love by leaving an ethical will, a document for your children and grandchildren that shares your beliefs, values, history and experiences. Nona did not actually realize that she had written an ethical will until she attended a series of lectures on the subject. When she shared hers with friends, they asked her to help them write theirs. Then she offered her services to her retirement community, and now works with some of the residents on their ethical wills and family histories.

44

Old age gave me the insight and opportunity to reach back and look at my life and how I lived it, and in some measure allowed my grandchildren to see me for who I was—not just the grandmother who gives presents.

Writing an ethical will has a cathartic value: it helps you in reliving your past as well as reminds you that to everything there is a season, and a time to every purpose under heaven. It also puts your life in perspective. Here is an excerpt from the ethical will I wrote for my children:

__I believe that protection__ and love of family is a core value. Being honest with myself and acting toward others as I would have them do unto me, means much more than trying to make an impression as someone important. I believe that there is a God, but I am not too sure how He/She helps me in my decisions and how I live my life…. but I hope for the better. I believe there is beauty all around me, and I try to make the world a better place by respecting that beauty.

__I hope that my behavior is ethical__ by being truthful and honest in my dealings with others. I go out of my way to help those I can. I believe in the freedom to speak my mind about injustices as I see them, and I believe that everyone has the right to his/her opinion even though I might abhor it, and I want that right to be returned to me. If I respect myself then it is not difficult for me to respect others, *no matter how offensive they might be. And I expect that others should respect me, no matter how I might offend them.*

I hope you teach your children *to respect themselves, others, and the world around them. There is not much more I can pass on to you, except my love for you.*

As expressed in her ethical will, these beliefs have guided Nona Chern's life. Her passion for justice and her ability to bounce back after setbacks have served her well in her later years. She also recognizes the importance of timing and learning when to reap and when to sow. Stretching a passage from *Ecclesiastes*, Nona shared one of her most important guiding principles,

There is a time for me to listen, there is a time for me to talk, and there is a time for me to light the way.

Her life has been a balance of all three.

46

Sara/Hannah Rigler, 84
An Indomitable Force

HAVEN'T WE ALL WONDERED WHAT ENABLED SOME people to survive the Holocaust while scores of others perished? Was it courage, determination or old-fashioned luck?

Sara/Hannah Rigler will tell you that it was a combination of all of the above. Her life story includes enormous bravery, resilience and, yes, good fortune. She has been resourceful: finding strangers to help her, turning them into friends and then embracing them as family. She has been loyal: keeping her promise to her own family to honor them by doing good in the world, and she has been dedicated: adding her sister Hannah's name to her own to memorialize her. (She was named Sara but some people call her Hannah; for purposes of this book, she wanted to use both names.) All of these qualities, which shaped her character as a young girl, continue to inform her life as an older woman.

I met Sara/Hannah through a friend. When she heard that I was writing a book exploring how older women have adapted to change and adversity throughout their long lives, she said, "You must meet S's cousin. She is a Holocaust survivor who walked away from a death march as a teenager and lived to tell her story." Then she gave me Sara/Hannah's memoir, *10 British Prisoners of War Saved My Life*, to read. Her experiences were both disturbing and miraculous. Although part of me dreaded hearing the details, at the same time, I was drawn to this woman who had experienced first hand what so many of us had only read about or viewed in movies.

Sara was born in Lithuania in 1928, three years after her sister Hannah, whose birthplace was Israel (called Palestine at the time). Although her parents had dreamed of settling in Tel Aviv, Sara/Hannah's grandmother missed her only daughter and wanted her nearby. Hannah was the adored, favored child—beautiful, docile and good. Her parents always compared Sara to her big sister, so rather than compete with her, Sara carved out her own niche as one of the neighborhood boys. She would hang out with them on their bicycles and they would race up the mountain on a narrow road with deep ravines on each side.

I was really daring. I was trying to be the boy my mother wanted but I did not get her approval that way either. She called me a plank with a hole. I did not get my period until I was sixteen.

Despite the sibling rivalry, Sara/Hannah has many pleasant memories of her childhood. She especially liked going to school and learning new things. Her family had a comfortable life in Shavel, a small town in northern Lithuania. Her father worked as a jobber of cigarettes initially and then opened a leather factory with his brother-in-law. Her mother had received a college education in St. Petersburg, Russia, unusual for women in those days. Observant Jews, they celebrated all the holidays as well as *Shabbat* (the Sabbath).

Life changed dramatically when the Russians and Germans came in 1940. Sara/Hannah was twelve years old. The Germans arrested all the men and forced the women and children into a ghetto. They had one hour to pack what they could carry. Sara/Hannah and her mother and sister spent two years there, waiting for her father to return. She remembers little of that time, except that they were always starving and there were no toilets, only outhouses.

In July of 1944, they took us. We wore two to three layers of clothing, leather coats and boots—in the hot summer. We put our bedding on our backs. We started in the morning and walked the whole day. We were very thirsty, so thirsty that we started drinking puddles in the street. We came to a holding place at the train station. We sat on our bundles, waiting to see what's next. My mother fainted. In the morning, they shoved us into cattle cars, destination unknown. Sixty people in a train. You had to relieve yourself in a bucket encircled by a sheet. I tried to erase all this from my mind: the stench, the heat, the meanness. They closed the doors. It was terrible. I do not know how many days we traveled on the train, maybe four or five.

We came to a place called Tiegenhoff where we were transferred to open trains on our journey to Stutthof, a concentration camp. Everything was dark:

dogs barking, guards dressed in black, people yelling, "Women on one side, men on the other side." Mothers calling for their children, running, screaming. It was a scene out of hell. Panic set in. We sat on sand. My mother took off her diamond watch and buried it in the sand but she held on to her diamond ring.

In the morning they took us to Stutthof, near Danzig. It was empty when we entered—except for mountains and mountains of shoes. Twenty feet tall. We had no idea what was going on there. Initially, we did have some luck: the Red Cross was coming to check the place because they heard it was an extermination camp and the Germans wanted to show that people were kept alive. We were one of the first transports not to be gassed. We stayed there three weeks. We slept on straw on the floor, keeping all our clothing in bundles with us.

We took our bundles to take a shower. Before entering the shower we left all our bundles and clothes. Men to one shower, women to another. Cold water, of course. We were examined internally to make sure that no one was hiding jewelry, but I do not remember that. My mother, sister and I received thin dresses, clogs and flannel underpants. My dress was white with a big red Magen David on the back. Then they gave us a number—not a tattoo. Mine was 54,384; it was pasted to my dress. From now on we were numbers, not people.

But we were not lucky, the three of us, after all. We only wore summer dresses and clogs on our feet. We stood and they counted us. We had to go to the bathroom together. Twenty toilets in a row. It was so hot, people were fainting. We stood for hours and hours. We got a tin of cold coffee for breakfast; lunch consisted of cabbage leaves in lukewarm water and some bread, and we had watery soup for supper. Three people to a bowl, a red metal bowl. The meanness…you cannot imagine the meanness.

As the front was moving, they moved us, from camp to camp. We started with a thousand women, now we were down to four hundred. This was a death march. I cannot even describe the conditions.

A German man with the kindest eyes approached me. He said, "Little girl, I live nearby. I can hide you." But he could not take my mother and sister so I did not go; he brought us bread instead. We each took one bite and then our mother slept on it in the barn. During the night someone stole the bread. It was a tragedy: our life depended on a piece of bread.

The last thing mother said was, "There is no place to run. We're on enemy territory. We have to stick together." But we were starving; I had to do something, so I said, "Give me the ring, I'm going to get us a bread."

49

I took the ring, ran out of the line and went into a barn. I waited to see who's going to come. I offered the ring to a kid and said, "Bring me a bread." He came back with the police and they chased me with pitchforks, yelling, "Jude, Jude" ("Jew, Jew"). People were watching the death march. I did not mind being killed but I did not want my mother to see. I do not know how I ran so fast: I was a starving bag of rags, my feet bleeding in the clogs. I looked like a wild animal. I ran into another barn and laid myself in a trough...

Sara/Hannah waited in the trough for hours. Later a British prisoner of war came in and told her they were no longer looking for her. And thus began her amazing rescue by ten British prisoners of war who brought her back to their camp and hid her in a hayloft. They tried to feed her, but for the first week, she got sick every time she ate because she had not eaten in so long. They put medicine on the ulcerated sores on her legs and used kerosene to eradicate her lice. She stayed in the barn for three weeks, which felt like an eternity, lying in the straw-lined trough as though it were a coffin and looking forward to meal times when the P.O.W.s brought her food and she had a little company.

After three weeks the P.O.W.s were evacuated; they had arranged for a Polish boy, who was told that Sara/Hannah was Polish too, to pick her up, but he never showed. Sara/Hannah knew she could not stay there so she left the barn, walked down the road, and found her way to another farm and asked for work. During the next few months she encountered various people in Poland and Germany as she tried to find her family and decide whether to go to Palestine or America. One day she met a girl from Shavel who had been with her mother and sister in the camps. She told her that her mother died of starvation and her sister died of typhoid and starvation on the very day of liberation. Devastated, she lost her will to live. What kept her going was the hope that her father was alive (he was not).

At her American relatives' urging, she decided to come to the United States. Since the quota for Lithuanians entering the U.S. was small, she knew it would take years to get a visa, so she tried another tack: a marriage-of-convenience to a rabbinic student. Once they arrived in America, they could divorce. This process took five months but that's how she landed in New York harbor on August 3, 1947. Her aunts and uncles greeted her and took a needy, lonely nineteen-year-old girl to Bushkill, Pennsylvania where they owned a small hotel.

They welcomed her by giving her dozens of boxes of candy. Each night she would sit alone in her room and eat chocolates. Her aunt and uncle realized how lonely and unhappy she was, so they decided to send her to Brooklyn to live with other relatives. They knew she needed a change and wanted her to receive a good education. Still lonely there, she spent her evenings writing letters to her dead mother.

Fortunately, the Dean of Girls at the high school she attended, whose family came from Lithuania, took an interest in Sara/Hannah. She found her a place to live with a war widow and her young son. This felt more like family. Eager to make up for lost time, Sara/Hannah finished high school in three terms and then completed nursing school, graduating at the top of her class.

Although she was obviously a highly motivated student, she still had time to date and met her husband Bill through mutual friends. A young struggling lawyer, he offered the compassion and kindness that she so needed. He later became a New York Supreme Court Judge. They were married four days short of sixty years. He died in September 2012 after a long battle with Crohn's disease. Sara/Hannah and Bill have two children, Lionel and Gail, and two grandchildren. Sara/Hannah loved being a mother and showered on her children all the affection and attention that she herself had missed.

Of her life in America, she writes in her book: "I came to America thinking the streets were paved with gold and I have found gold in a husband who has understood that a survivor of the Holocaust has a legacy of agony and sorrow that can overwhelm even the strongest without the love and support of a special man. There were times when I wished for death, but I am a survivor and I know that life is the ultimate gift. The human heart can and does break, but it mends when healed by joy and love."

Because she had vowed to her own family that if she survived the Holocaust she would do good in the world, she became involved in New York politics. She was elected New York State Committee Woman representing forty thousand constituents. Some of the highlights of her career include creating Senior Citizen Centers in Brooklyn and rallying for Soviet Jews to immigrate to the United States.

In 1994 she retired from the world of paid employment and renewed her efforts as a volunteer. Much of her volunteer work revolves around her promise to her mother, father and sister to keep alive their memories and those of other victims of the Holocaust. She served as Chairwoman of the

Center for Holocaust Studies, Documentation and Research in Brooklyn and has also been involved in many capacities in the Jewish Heritage Museum in New York since it opened in 1997.

Over the years, Sara/Hannah tried to re-connect with the British prisoners-of-war who saved her. A complicated story of failed attempts, her persistence finally paid off: they had a reunion in London in 1972, after she spent twenty-four years searching for them. In 1988 the BBC profiled the story of her survival and the ten men who risked their lives to save her. The following year Yad Vashem, a memorial to the Holocaust in Jerusalem, honored them.

In early 2012 Sara/Hannah and Bill moved into a retirement community near Dallas to be near their daughter because of Bill's failing health. At the time of our interviews, they had lived there about four months, so she was still adjusting to the new environment, especially to a string of over one-hundred-degree days.

Today Sara/Hannah occupies herself with many activities. She either swims or goes to chair exercises every day. Sometimes she walks the halls, because they are air-conditioned. She reads the newspaper and a few magazines. She remains active at the Museum of Jewish Heritage in New York City: she serves on the board, she lectures for them, and they sell her book in their shop. One of the pleasures of her present life—and a lifesaver for her throughout the years—has been the support of her close friends.

A good friend is a gift that you give to yourself—Not the phony "How are you?" I appreciate that I can talk to someone who is really interested in me and vice versa. I speak to two women twice a day. I have known them for years. Nesse I met in kindergarten. Lotte I met in 1976 on a bus to Washington, D.C. to rally for Soviet Jewry. She is the most positive person I know. She has had a hard life—she was a seamstress— but she does not complain. She is a treasure. A true friendship is real wealth.

I'm grateful for old friends. And I'm grateful for new, younger friends too. You can be old at fifty and you can be young at eighty-five. I have many younger friends. I love them. I'm their marriage advisor. I like younger people, who are "with it" and who do not mind associating with older people. I think young.

In our culture there is a tremendous emphasis on money and material things. It's what you do with the money that counts. I had a dress for thirty years. A "friend" said to me, "I saw what you're wearing before." I said, "Yeah, you'll see it again too! As long as it's clean and I'm comfortable in it, I'll continue wearing it. I do not need to impress anyone."

There is such an emphasis on clothing, and not enough emphasis on values: feeling for someone else. If I see an older person unable to walk, I help them. We are a selfish society, absorbed with our homes and ourselves. We stress material values. People do not value other people. We're losing what's important. I have a friend who built a whole town in Israel called Chazor. Fifty-eight thousand people live there and work and thrive. She is very wealthy but she wears a simple little gold wedding band. I appreciate that and take pride in her accomplishments. You do not need a lot of friends—just a few close friends. Mine have been a tremendous support for me over the years.

Besides building a strong support system, I wondered what other advice Sara/Hannah has for younger women to help them prepare for their later years.

You must feel good about yourself. I do not care what you do as long as you can take care of yourself and take pride in yourself. You have to think well of yourself. You're not a shmatte. *You need a goal. What do you want to do with your life? To reach that goal, you do whatever you have to do, even if it's cleaning houses. You have to be proud of yourself. Think: I'm a human being; I'm entitled to this and this and this. Some women are just happy getting married and having kids and that's it. Others have different goals.*

Live your life. Know what your real values are. Do not ever owe anyone anything. Live so you do not go to sleep and worry: how will I pay that bill? No one cares if you eat steak or chopped meat. An honest life is a difficult one. Live according to your means. Go to sleep worry-free about bills. Everyone has to decide what they want in life and then you follow it or try to follow it.

Although Sara/Hannah's father was Orthodox and today she belongs to a conservative *shul*, going to synagogue is not what means the most to her about Judaism. It is living Jewish values.

The most important thing is being a mensch *and I have tried to be a* mensch *my whole life. I have never lied. Never. I try to do the right thing. I have tried to show my kids by example. That's what my father always used to say and I follow his advice to this day.*

Sara/Hannah Rigler has had a long, difficult life and has overcome horrors and hardships that most of us will never know. Is she happy today?

I'm very grateful that I survived, that I have children. I'm the only one from the whole family who endured. But am I happy? I'm alone. I lost everybody and now Bill is gone. But I do not want anyone to feel sorry for me. The only one who can feel sorry for me is me. Happiness is really within you. I like to be with people I like, people who accept me and are interesting. Relationships are very important to me.

But I do not wear my history on my sleeve. I was always known as HH, Happy Hannah. I never say I'm a Holocaust survivor. It's not my title. I do not take pride in it. It was very unfortunate, but it's not my claim to fame. I opened the first senior citizen center in Brooklyn. That, I'm proud of. The Holocaust, this was a tragedy. I'm sad about it. I lost everyone. I do not want to talk about it and I do not want anyone to feel sorry for me.

Happiness, it's a very big thing. For me, if my kids are all right, then I'm happy. Now I'm grateful I can get up in the morning on my own two feet, that I can swim in the pool, that I can think for myself, and talk to my friends. I thank God every morning.

The Epilogue of Sara/Hannah Rigler's book summarizes her life well. In it she writes, "I was given the gift of life. Through me, my mother, father and sister live on…I am a living example that it is very hard to extinguish the soul—the Nazis, Russians, Lithuanians all tried—but as long as I'm alive, and even after death, they cannot kill the love I feel for the people who have touched my life and I theirs."

I am a woman who never gives up. I have stared into the abyss of death at sixteen and now…still keep my pact with my family and friends never to forget them and to do good in the world.

I am resilient, persistent, practical, compassionate, intelligent and lucky. Hannah and I have touched many lives and by surviving, I have shown that even in the midst of great evil there is goodness—even in the midst of great sorrow there is the possibility of happiness—even in a world of indifference there is love and the gift of life.

Estelle Bloom, 90
Committed to Activism

ESTELLE BLOOM ALWAYS HAD A STRONG SOCIAL conscience. When she graduated from high school, her father bought her a shirred beaver coat. Although she thought it was beautiful, she felt uncomfortable wearing it—and did not for years—because most of the people she knew could not afford one. Ever sensitive to the underdog and those not treated fairly, she is a living example of a highly regarded Jewish value: *tikkun olam*. This Hebrew phrase suggests humanity's shared responsibility to "heal, repair, and transform the world." In many ways Estelle did her part as a younger woman and continues to do so today.

Her passion for making a difference and speaking out against discrimination has kept her vital for more than nine decades. At the same time, the stability of a strong, loving extended family and the strength of long-term female friendships gave her a secure foundation from which to venture out and make her mark; their support in times of tragedy has helped her recover and rebound.

An acquaintance introduced me to Estelle with this explanation: "She is an old friend of my mother's. They were active in the peace movement together and she is just fabulous. She is ninety, Jewish, and still volunteers at a Catholic charity outreach." When I spoke to Estelle for the first time, she told me that she had lived an ordinary life and had not done anything spectacular, although she has plenty of friends who are doing great things. As we began the interviewing process, it became clear how remarkable her ordinary life was.

Estelle grew up in Washington Heights, a neighborhood in the northern section of Manhattan near the end of the George Washington Bridge. Raised with her younger brother in a two-bedroom apartment in a neighborhood of mixed religions, Estelle was surrounded by cousins, grandparents, and aunts and uncles. As a child she suffered from mastoiditis, an inflammation of the spaces within the mastoid bone behind the ear at the base of the skull, which often creates an infection in the middle ear. She was quite ill and needed to be hospitalized many times, sometimes for as long as a month. She had surgery several times, coming home with her head wrapped in bandages. No antibiotics existed at that time, so her infections probably were life threatening. Being in the hospital created anxiety for her, especially one time when her mother had pneumonia and could not visit her.

I always felt comfortable growing up. My dad was in the wholesale meat business, I went to good schools, and we had a nice park near us. My family was not affected by the Depression or the crash, because we did not have money in the stock market. I was very fortunate that I never felt personally deprived. Even as a young girl, this created a little guilt in me: so many people experienced difficult times and I was so comfortable.

As we shall see, these early experiences helped determine the kind of woman she would become. Easing her own guilt initially motivated her to help the less fortunate and those discriminated against. Later, her activism became a passion and a way of life.

The early friendships she established influenced her life as well. As a teenager, she and seven friends formed an organization called Senippah (happiness spelled backwards with one S). They met every Friday to talk about their lives, with a special emphasis on boys. They hung out together and went to the movies. They remained friends as they married, as their husbands served in the army, as they raised their children and then, as their husbands died, one by one. They all live or lived in the New York/New Jersey area. Today four women remain. Because most of them do not drive, they have stopped meeting in person, but they still stay in touch by phone. They remain Estelle's dear friends.

Born Jewish, Estelle considers herself Jewish in her heart. She rarely set foot in a synagogue, although her brother did have a Bar Mitzvah; her parents felt that was important because he was a boy. When she did go to services with friends, she enjoyed them. Passover was the most meaningful holiday to her and her family when she was growing up. She, in particular, could relate to a holiday about freedom. When she had her own children, she continued the tradition of hosting annual Seders and liked to include special readings, such as quotes from Anne Frank or the Freedom Fighters of Germany.

Estelle started college after high school but then dropped out to marry at age twenty. She met her husband when she was a senior in high school and he, a senior in college. She noticed this good-looking guy reading a book on the beach and with the encouragement of her friends, went over to talk to him *en masse*. They dated for a few years before he enlisted in the army. Once they married, he was sent to Officers' Training School in Florida. She accompanied him and became pregnant almost immediately. When he shipped out, she moved in with her parents. He did not come home until their daughter was two years old.

On his return, they lived with her parents because they could not find an apartment to rent. After a couple of years they heard about Levittown, a new community on Long Island for veterans. She felt terrible about signing the rental lease because it contained a "discrimination clause" that prohibited people of color from living there. As soon as she moved in, she joined the committee that worked to change the clause. Eventually, the committee succeeded in having it removed. Estelle and her husband later bought a house in Levittown and found it a wonderful place to raise their two daughters and son. The children grew up in a community with streets full of other children and good schools.

During this time, her activism flourished. She joined B'nai B'rith and the Anti-Defamation League. She fought book banning, worked for better schools, and went door-to-door to support a library for the community. She boycotted grapes, picketed a nuclear plant, and went on peace marches. She also traveled to Washington, D.C. to support Martin Luther King, Jr., belonged to CORE, and picketed the five and dime in Levittown in sympathy with the civil rights movement in the South.

I was always bothered by a feeling of separation. Growing up, I lived in one neighborhood and two miles away was Harlem. I could not figure out why one neighborhood should be white and another black. There was something that felt wrong about it. I was also aware of the economic differences between people and that bothered me too.

I never put my life on the line and I never crossed a picket line, but if I felt there was a need, I had to be part of making a change. That was always something I believed. I had to be involved. If I felt there were injustices I had to find a way to make the world better...Because I was so comfortable, I never thought of doing anything else. I was not doing drastic things but I always had a social conscience. I cannot quite define what created this fervor in me. My family was not politically active at all. In fact, my mother was disturbed when she saw me handing out literature for the American Labor Party at a subway stop when I was fourteen. They were good people, but I wished they were more active. Maybe reading the newspapers, having a sense that everyone should be as comfortable as I was...I cannot pinpoint an incident that made me an activist.

Estelle received a degree in education and then taught developmentally disabled children during the time her own children were still at home. Just as they were in the process of moving out, her husband had a heart attack. He died after a week in the hospital. Forty-five years old at the time, she was in shock. No bereavement groups existed back then, but she did go for counseling. After a couple of weeks, she went back to work; that helped ease the pain. She reflects on that time:

It would have been nice if my husband and I could have grown old together. We married so young, and the children were born so quickly. Then we were active bringing them up, and financially we both had to work. I was so busy saving the world that I kind of got lost.... He never really reached his potential as a person. Truth is, I would like to do some of it over and I cannot. We wanted a chance to be together after the children grew up; I miss the fact that we did not have that time together.

After her husband's death, Estelle went back to school to earn a master's degree. She had another caring partner for many years, until his death fifteen years ago. She remains close to his children to this day. During that time she experienced another trauma. Her mother, who was a vital eighty-nine at the time, spent the night at Estelle's because she had a dentist appointment the next day in her neighborhood. During the night, she fell down the stairs; she died in the hospital a few days later. The doctors believe she had a stroke and later determined that she also had a burst appendix. It took Estelle a long time to recover from this incident because she felt so responsible. Again, she went to her friends and family for support and also benefited from counseling.

Estelle continued working with developmentally disabled children during the day and taught English as a Second Language at night. She retired at age seventy only because she broke her hip and could no longer teach in a classroom. Upon retirement, she continued teaching English as a Second Language and began working with a Catholic charities outreach program three days a week.

Estelle still gives her time there, driving seven miles from her home to the center. As a core worker, she interviews people, assesses their needs, and facilitates their receiving the help they need, working along side a wonderful staff. She recently signed up for a refresher course to become an Adult Literacy Tutor. She also belongs to a book group, goes to lectures at the library, and sees her friends. She enjoys the city's museums and theater. She is in constant contact with her brother and sister-in-law and their family, who live in Albuquerque, and she still lives in the same house in which she raised her family in Levittown; most nights she cooks dinner for herself. She has an active, full life that appears almost idyllic until she reveals that her oldest daughter Marcea died a few months ago.

Estelle did not know until recently that her husband's family had the BRCA gene for breast or ovarian cancer, a gene that her daughter inherited. Marcea fought cancer for four years, never complaining. While she was sick, she continued teaching school, belonged to a theater troupe, did yoga, and maintained a busy life. She taught until the end of the term before her death in the fall of 2012.

The biggest shock was that she had all the symptoms but the doctors did not recognize them. By the time they identified them, she had Stage 4 cancer. She lived to be in her sixties, but I wanted more for her. I wanted her to be as fortunate as I am and live into her nineties. I was always a worrier, but I never expected this to happen.

She'll always be a piece of me and my life and I'll always mourn her. My life goes on, but every day I think of her. It's extraordinary to experience a daughter's death. I'm not really through it. This is my own personal loss, my own personal mourning. But I must say, everyone—my son, my other daughter, the rest of my family—has been there for me. Having my family involved, going through this together, certainly helps.

After my husband died, I said to someone that the shape of your life changes after a death and it can never be the same as it was before. I feel the same way now. I have led a fortunate life but this is something that I never thought would happen. Up until now, everything has gone in order. Losses change who you are.

Estelle's other children—both social workers—her four grandchildren, and four great grandchildren have always been a joy to her, and they have been a special comfort to her during the last few difficult months. She took four weeks off from her volunteer work and then returned to a full schedule. Although she has some physical problems—a heart condition and a bad knee, both treated with medication—she still drives and keeps in touch with her old friends.

When I asked about what she felt contributed to her longevity and vitality, she said,

It's not the years but what you do with the long life that counts. I'm happy I could do all the things I did. I wanted to right some of the wrongs. I had to make a contribution. I'm doing it because there is no other way that I could live. I need to be able to contribute. I need to have friends. I care about my family. I would like to change some of the world, but I feel like my little piece of the world is pretty good. Yet I have to stay active; it's like earning my keep. It's the way I am. It fulfills me. It's been my way of being ever since I can remember. I don't feel I do much. I don't put my life on the line, but I feel sad for all the suffering in the world.

While Estelle recognizes that the life she has led does not suit everyone, she does offer some advice for younger women, no matter what their path.

First, have a little mazel (good luck). Keep active physically and mentally. Be involved in the world. Be open to support. Find people who care for you. That's what I needed. Be able to enjoy your friends and family, and good

health. Make adjustments when necessary. Don't look back and think about what you should have done. Enjoy the moment you're going through right now and try to live your life so you don't have a lot of regrets.

Get up and do something every day. You need to be involved. Do the things you enjoy. Keep learning. Find someone you can talk to. If I could not do volunteer work, I would be satisfied to read and see my friends. Have the people you love around you and have them be well. When that's not happening, your whole life becomes different. When all is okay and you have taken care of yourself, then try to keep yourself active, have a sense of self worth.

It's scary being this old, yet I feel lucky. I have always been active. I like to read, take an art course. You hope you'll be able to handle what comes your way. At some point you make peace with dying. It's not on my mind a lot, but I think it might be why I try to keep so busy. When I'm home with bad weather, I read, I'm on phone, I organize things. During (storm) Sandy, I had no electricity for a week. I would go to a friend's house who had electricity during the day and come home to sleep at night. I had no phone or television for a month. I couldn't go to work because I didn't have gas in my car. Compared to others, I got away easily.

That's the thing: Even with all that's happened to me, I feel like I led a privileged life. There are so many people who are struggling in this world. Each person has his or her own personal trials, and when you're floundering, you don't see some of the wonderful things in your life. I know it sounds corny but stop and smell the roses. I did not struggle a lot financially but I had lots of sad moments. The support of my friends and four generations of my family helped me recover. I've led an ordinary life, but I've been lucky in many ways.

Bernice Levy Klein, 88
Family First

BERNICE LEVY KLEIN (BEA) GREW UP IN Nogales, Arizona, a border town with a cosmopolitan flair in the late twenties and thirties. In the days before airplanes, it served as the west coast entrance to Mexico and was the largest importer of produce from Mexico. Ranchers, movie stars, Mexicans and Anglos—and several Jewish families—filled the area. Bea married the first Jewish man she met to whom she was not related and they moved to his hometown of Las Cruces in the late 1940s. She has lived there sixty-six years.

Bea represents an important segment of her generation: women who devoted themselves to their husbands and children, and either worked or did volunteer work. These were not high-achieving career women; these women's lives revolved around their home. Even though women like Bea might have led "ordinary" lives as housewives and mothers, something in their earlier decades must have prepared them for an active, fulfilling late age. In Bea's case, the importance of family made a mark. Both her mother and her father had a strong positive influence on her. She perpetuated their values when raising her own children. More recently, Bea is beginning to reap the rewards of her years of nurturing her family as the tables turn and they support her in her later years.

Today Bea is involved in her synagogue and is also active in the Democratic Party, the Arts Council, the symphony, and the Progressive Voters Association. She volunteers for the Slightly Used Boutique that raises money for a home for homeless women and outfits them in clothing so they can apply for jobs. She loves sports and in the last year she attended fifteen basketball games at New Mexico State University. She lives alone in the sprawling ranch house that she and her husband built to raise their three children.

I met Bea through a childhood friend from Wisconsin. Bea was her mother's best friend. My friend told me, "From the moment I met Bea, she reminded me of my mother's friends in Racine. They were really all like aunts to me. I felt the same way about her—that she was part of my family and that I had always known her." I felt similarly after spending an afternoon with Bea. She was warm and familiar, yet feisty and frank. She spoke her mind freely and shared her passions openly.

In a wide-ranging conversation, Bea told me that her parents were born in New York but ended up in Nogales because her father was tubercular. They moved west for a drier climate, right after Bea's older sister Helen was born. They chose Nogales because her mother's brother lived there; he owned an army/navy story. Even though few Jewish families lived in town, Bea never experienced any antisemitism. Their family had a high profile because they owned a popular restaurant. People of all backgrounds came into Levy's Border Café and would ask, "Mrs. Levy, do you have the chicken soup with the golf balls?"

The restaurant became Bea's home. She ate three meals a day there and hung out after school. For a while, they lived in a hotel above the restaurant and then moved to an apartment and eventually, to a small house. Bea's mother inspired Bea and everyone else in town. She could "read" people and she told things as they were. Friends and acquaintances—in and outside of the family—adored her, as did Bea.

Bea's father also had a strong impact on her but for different reasons. When he was not working, he loved to attend sporting events. A boxer as a young man, he would take Bea to Tucson to see the University of Arizona games. Much as she resented being *schlepped* to games at first, she cherished their time together and her father eventually instilled a love of sports in her that remains to this day.

Bea's sister, on the other hand, had no interest in sports. She married very young into a large Jewish family. As years went by, they prospered, traveled widely, and collected art.

No synagogue existed in Nogales, so Bea's family celebrated the holidays at home and lit *Shabbat* candles on Friday night. For the High Holidays they drove to Tucson, sixty-seven miles north on a two-lane highway, to attend services.

I loved the summers best. We would load the family up in the car, cooling our faces with wet towels, and drive to California and rent an apartment between Ocean Park and Venice Pier. That was our beach. My future husband's family did the same thing. I met Howard on the beach when I was fourteen. We had a long distance romance. He went to college and then in the army. When he got out, we married. I was twenty-one.

In 1946, the newlyweds moved to Las Cruces, where Howard's family lived. When her sister heard of their move, she said, "Oh, Bea, that's wonderful. They have a university there. You can continue your education." Bea was not interested in more schooling. "I wanted to be a housewife," she said. Bea and Howard raised their three children there. Howard's family owned a furniture store on Main Street and they participated in community activities, sporting events, and political causes. Bea joined in everything they did. At one point, her father-in-law served as mayor. Bea loves to tell the following story to show how strong their convictions were.

My mother had a heart attack on November 8, 1960, the day Kennedy was elected. She was in the ambulance going to the hospital and asked the ambulance driver to swing by the polls so she could vote. She said, "Howard will be so mad if I don't vote for Kennedy!"

Bea worked as a homemaker and a volunteer while she raised her family. When her son was six, they helped start a Sunday school in their home, and then began offering services there. As the congregation grew, they moved to larger quarters: the Elks Club, the library, and eventually to their own building. People from White Sands came for services, as did soldiers. After her children left home, Bea opened a gift shop with a partner and worked there for fifteen years. She had to close it when her husband became ill. He developed cancer in his fifties and was sick on and off for eighteen years. He died two months after their fiftieth wedding anniversary in 1996.

He had many different surgeries but I was not living with a sick man. He was just a man who had cancer. He never complained. Whenever he was well, we kept going. Whatever involvements he had, I had. Las Cruces was very social and we were very social too. But that was the hardest time in my marriage: Living with his illness, I developed health problems myself from nerves.

Becoming a widow at seventy-three has brought some changes to Bea's life. For one thing, she feels content to stay home. Although she remains active and engaged in her community, she does not have the same need to go-go-go as she did when she was younger. Some days she is satisfied to read and watch television at home.

In Bea's day, it was unusual for a woman to eat alone in a public place and in fact, she had never done it. After her husband died, she ate by herself in a restaurant for the first time. She happened to have an hour between two doctor's appointments and did not have time to run home for lunch.

I told the owner that this was the first time I ate in a restaurant by myself and he pulled up a chair and sat with me. It was strange for me to do it. I saw people that I knew. I ate alone. It was OK, but I would rather eat at home. I fix three meals a day at home.

68

As someone who was always very active, Bea has had to learn to accept her physical limitations as she ages. She has spinal stenosis and sciatica.

Not being able to do the things I want to do physically is the hardest part of getting old. I see weeds and I can't pull them. If I do a little bit in the garden, I pay for it. I love to walk and used to walk in the neighborhood and meet my neighbors, but I can't do that anymore. I walk ten minutes and my legs turn to rubber. That makes me sad. I take ibuprofen. My doctor wants to do epidural injections for my back. If I can get along with a couple of pills a day, I would rather do that. But I'm bent over. I used to go to the symphony and see these old people bent over and I would thank God that I'm not like that. Well, I'm getting like that.

Even though her physical restrictions affect her every day, she does not let them get her down. She uses nature as an antidote to depression: She cannot walk far outside, but her positive, appreciative attitude keeps her spirits up.

I live every day as if it's going to be a good one. You have to take each day as it comes and make the most of it. Sometimes I get a little sad but I have never been depressed. I will not allow myself to be depressed. I have had a good life and I'm going to continue to have a good life. I'm lucky. I do not want to die but I'm not afraid of it. Sometimes I'm lonely. When I feel that way, I go out and focus on the mountains. They are my sanctuary. I look at the mountains and say, "Thank you, God, that I'm here." I feel grateful for each day.

Bea is not sure what accounts for her longevity. Her father died at fifty-eight, her mother at sixty-eight, and her sister at seventy-three, so she has outlived her immediate family. Clearly, the answer does not lie in the genes. Even though she is eighty-eight, she feels like she is seventy. This is a typical response of the women I have interviewed. None of them feels they are their chronological age. They all feel like they're younger.

My mind does not realize how old my body is, but my body is changing. My mind is beginning to accept that the body is old and aching but, frankly, I'm shocked that I'm as old as I am.

I asked Bea what advice she had for women my age and younger. This is what she said:

Be active and be productive. Do for others. Do not feel sorry for yourself and do not be envious. In Nogales we were the poorer ones. I worked in the restaurant. My sister hated it. She became well to do. I never envied what she had. She was generous to me, but I was never jealous. My husband and I had a happy home. Of course, there were fights, but our home was open to our kids and their friends and all of our friends. We built the house of our dreams, later we put the pool in. We did things here, we had a lot of parties, we sat and talked. People don't converse any more. They're always playing with their computer gadgets. We have lost the art of conversation and that's too bad.

I have friends of all different backgrounds and I love interacting with all kinds of people. I respect other people's beliefs and their ways of life. I'll go to their churches as long as they don't put their beliefs on me. I don't tolerate extreme beliefs in any religion, including my own.

Now, after living alone for the sixteen years since her husband's death, Bea will experience a major transition. Her daughter and son-in-law, who live in San Diego, are in the process of moving in with her. This trend is becoming more common as younger people experience financial setbacks. Fortunately, Bea has space for them, but more important for the family dynamics is her positive attitude. She acknowledges that it will be a huge adjustment for her and for them, but she is actually looking forward to the change.

I love my family. You do what you can to help them. But I'm concerned about them; this move is a bigger shock to their lives than to mine. I'll go about my life as before...We'll just take one day at a time. I can't see what the future will bring, but I'm very happy about it.

I'm alone and I'm not getting younger. I always loved having a full house. This house has so many memories—walls and walls of photos, books, and mementos. Now I will have someone to share my memories with and the house will be alive again.

70

Elizabeth Norman, 102
Love of Learning

At Liz Norman's ninety-fifth birthday party, her thirty-year-old granddaughter Michelle gave a tribute to her that illuminated the strength of character that she felt played a role in her grandmother's longevity. She said, "Her spirit is epitomized by her fierce independence, her penuriousness for herself but her generosity for others, her fair-mindedness, her stellar intellect, her techno-color memory, her desire to both learn and to teach, and her ability to tell and laugh at a good joke."

As we shall see, this strength of character surfaced throughout her long life and continues to serve her well as she prepares to celebrate her one hundred and second birthday. I did not mark that milestone with her, but Liz has been in the background of my life for many years. Her son Michael and my husband met in junior high school and have maintained their friendship on and off for more than sixty years. I remember hearing stories about Liz but did not have an opportunity to meet her until the fall of 2012 when I went to Los Angeles to interview two women for this book.

In marathon interview sessions, Liz regaled me with stories about her family and her long life. Michelle was right: her mind is sharp, her memory is excellent, and she is tireless. As she recounted anecdotes about her life, what came through was the driving force of her personality, her determination, and her desire and ability to use her love of learning to help her adapt to transition and change.

Born in 1911, Liz grew up in Philadelphia, the oldest of five children. According to the Jewish tradition of naming newborns for the dead, her parents named her Eeta (in Yiddish) after her grandfather Isaac who died two months before she was born. The attending doctor, however, needed an English name to certify her birth in City Hall. They could not think of a name so he decided that since he admired Queen Elizabeth, they should give her that name. Hence, her English name, which was not a common name for Jewish children in those days.

Liz's father was a wood worker and specialized in making trunks. In the evening he enlisted his children to paper the inside of the trunks. Her mother, "a woman of the kitchen," was a good seamstress and made all the children's clothing. She had to shop for food every day because no refrigeration existed then.

We were not starving but we certainly were not rich. I do not remember my mother ever saying to my father, "Sam why don't you try something else? Work a little harder?" (as I did with my husband)

My mother was a good cook. In those days you would go to the Jewish butcher and buy a pound of meat. Then they would give you the bones so you could make soup, and eat whatever was left on the bones or marrow. Very often they gave you the heart and the lungs for free because nobody wanted them. My mother took those home and would fry some onions and grind it all together, and then make dough and turn it into knishes. I never knew until I got married that you could buy noodles in the store.

Liz's mother, who was very shy, only spoke Yiddish; she refused to learn English so Liz's grandmother took her to school and communicated with the teachers. A bright student, Liz started first grade at age five, graduated from eighth grade at twelve and from high school at sixteen.

In high school I signed up for the academic course—until my mother's sister, Aunt Rose, came. She spoke English so I told her I was taking an academic course. She said, "What's a Jewish girl doing with academics?" I replied, "I can be a teacher." "A teacher?" she queried. "Teachers become old maids. A nice Jewish girl becomes a bookkeeper." She insisted that I change to the commercial course, which I did. A half-year later I defied my family and changed back to the academic course, studying Latin.

While in high school, she also attended Gratz College, a leading institute of Jewish learning, two nights a week and Sunday mornings to learn how to teach Hebrew. Twice she won the best student award. Following high school, Liz went to what was then called a normal school, a two-year program to train people to teach at the elementary school level. Although she became a licensed teacher, she could not find a job in 1929, due to the depression and a glut of unemployed teachers. But she was able to find a job teaching Hebrew after school. In fact, the principal who hired her became her husband Max. They dated for three years before they married and were together for forty-two years until his death at seventy-four. Liz explains how well they complimented each other.

Max came from a middle class family in Russia. He had a good education and spoke several languages. He was an aggressive businessman; actually, he was aggressive in many ways. I'm not. I'm hardworking but you need more than just the ability to work hard. You have to have the ability to approach people and to sell yourself first. Max could do a lot of that and did. I was never good with people, never, but I was the driving force behind each of our ventures.

They waited for five or six years to have children because they could not afford them. Liz did not feel they could make enough money to support a family with only their Hebrew school positions, so they opened a drug store (along with the teaching jobs). Then they dabbled in real estate. She would find the property and tell her husband, "Go and negotiate." Next she went to pharmacy school, a four-year program, so she could fill prescriptions. As their last venture they bought a camp in the Pocono Mountains in Pennsylvania. She never worked so hard in her life.

Four wells had to be dug, four hundred feet deep! We had to solicit campers and staff continually. I went to the docks and bought fruit and vegetables; we purchased kosher chickens and meat in Philadelphia and had them brought in by truck. During rest hour I tutored the kids for their Bar Mitzvah or in reading; the rest of the time I ran the kitchen. Whatever we made in the camp we had to put back in. After eighteen years, I had to get rid of that camp. I was never so happy to sell it.

Liz and Max had three boys; their youngest son died suddenly at twenty-two months. They never found out exactly what happened to him.

She remembers that their pediatrician came over two afternoons in a row to check him because he was not feeling well. After examining him, he said he was fine. Still concerned, they took him to the hospital the next day and he died that evening. Talking about him—fifty years later—brings tears to her eyes.

I could not live without him. He was the most beautiful child I ever saw. I decided I could do two things: continue to teach Hebrew, but that's only from four to eight p.m. What would I do all day? Or I could teach school. I decided to go back to school to prepare for my master's and teacher's exams. I worked for twenty-two years in the schools, taught elementary for ten, received my master's and became a school psychologist, and then did that for eight years. This gave me a purpose for living.

Max died in November 1974. He had a heart condition for many years so his death was not a surprise. Not one to dwell on her feelings, Liz responded by moving into action. Michelle, her first grandchild, was born the following April and in November Liz uprooted herself and moved to California. She was sixty-three at the time and retired with "considerable money." Several things called her west. Her two sons, both highly accomplished professionals, had relocated to California, and her sister and her husband also lived there. They graciously included her in their social circle; their friends became hers.

Liz felt strongly that she did not want to be a burden to her children, so she obtained her own apartment. Then she began taking courses at Emeritus College, a program of Santa Monica College serving older adults. She took classes in Shakespeare, repertory theater, Yiddish classics and current movies. She stopped driving many years ago because she has only peripheral vision in one eye, but she refused to take cabs because they were too expensive. People were shocked when she told them that she rode the bus. "Buses are for people," they would tell her. "Well, I'm people," she would retort. "I don't object to sitting with people." She rode the bus until she turned one hundred.

Liz also belonged to a number of book clubs. As her friends have aged and died, so have the book clubs. One club that lasted twenty years broke up just last year. Her daughter-in-law Susan, a professional flutist, has enhanced her life as well. She has offered her many opportunities to go to concerts. Susan also encouraged her to be a hands-on grandmother and help raise her two children. Liz, in turn, vowed never to say "no" to Susan and continues to be an integral part of their lives.

Although she did some traveling with Max, her real travels began when she moved to California and started touring with her sister and brother-in-law; sometimes they took as many as twenty trips a year. She has been to every place in the world that she ever wanted to go, including six extended trips to Israel. A staunch Zionist, she set up a scholarship in memory of the son she lost at Technion University, an Israeli world-renowned research university.

At one hundred and one, she moved into a retirement community. She was not happy about the move because she values her independence, but she agreed to it because it gave her sons a sense of comfort that she was not living alone. When she moved into the smaller space, she had to give away close to one thousand books. She selected twenty of her favorite titles to take with her. Among the books she kept were dictionaries in English, Hebrew, French, Spanish, Italian, German, and Yiddish; Irving Howe's *The World of Our Fathers*; the daily prayer book, and the *High Holy Days Prayer Book*.

Liz enjoys good health and her heart remains strong. She has difficulty walking and standing due to a hip replacement twenty years ago. She has some hearing loss, which makes conversation on the telephone difficult, and she is a breast cancer survivor. She had a very small cancer when she was one hundred, which was removed and radiated. But as she will tell you, "For a woman my age, I'm in perfect good health."

Now her days are different. After breakfast, she reads *The New York Times* and the *Los Angeles Times* so she can debate current events with her grandchildren and their spouses. She continues to read *The New Yorker* every week as she has done for years. Her afternoons and evenings are spent going to a yoga or an exercise class or one of the many programs offered. She is particularly interested in programs with historical, medical and political themes.

I wondered what drives her to continue learning at her age.

Why would I read The New Yorker *or the paper everyday? Maybe twenty people in the whole building come in to read those papers. Two or three people are there when I'm there and that's all. We cannot pull together a book club with ten people and there are four hundred people living here. I sometimes read as much as three books a week. Why? Years ago my principal asked me whether I wanted to be the smartest girl in the cemetery. I don't. I had to improve my education and in Philadelphia you needed those levels in order to move up. I needed to make more money, but now...*

I'm just lucky. I always had a goal in life I had to achieve. First Max and I had to make a little money to get out of poverty. Second of all, we had to live in relation to our economic state. And it's always been my goal to learn more: to begin to study French when I'm in my eighties, to take five courses at the Emeritus College when I'm in my nineties—those are aspirations that very few people have. But I love to learn. That's my character. I have wanted to learn from the time I went to the public library at eight years old and I have been reading books my entire life.

Everybody asks Liz what she believes contributes to her longevity. She thinks good genes did play a part although she has lived longer than everyone in her family. She was also the first one in her family to realize the importance of an education as a means to break out of the class in which she was born. Her sister told her once that she set a standard for the family. As she said earlier, she always had a goal—to move beyond being poor—and that goal motivated her for years. She never cared about wearing expensive clothing or sitting in the fifth row at the theater. She never even wanted to be rich; she wanted to escape poverty.

Her life as an older woman, in many ways, reflects the choices she made at a younger age. By working hard, obtaining a good education, and being frugal in the past, she was able to reap the benefits later. She could contribute to causes and organizations she believed in. She could travel wherever she wanted to go. While she no longer has the desire to travel, as a voracious reader, she escapes and continues to learn through books. She remains a role model for her four grandchildren. Michelle, for one, wants to emulate the attributes that have contributed to Liz's long life: "her penchant for hard work, her commitment to giving back to the community, her quest for knowledge, her devotion to family, and her eternal optimism."

As the matriarch of the California Norman clan and the proud great grandmother of four little ones, Liz believes in living in the present. She does not think about death. Right now she is focused on her next birthday party. Family and friends are coming from all over. Tributes and toasts will abound.

It's funny. Nobody was invited but they're all coming. I don't know what they're going to do with everybody. It's turning into a big party. They all want to be there to see what it looks like to be one hundred and two.

Joan Lorch Staple, 90
Challenges and Changes

J OAN LORCH STAPLE HAS RETIRED FROM HER career as a
biology researcher and teacher but her life at ninety is far from passive.
She exercises every day—biking, walking, yoga, and floor exercises. She
reads books on a Kindle, lectures on her life to senior centers, attends the
Unitarian Universalist Church, and plays Scrabble once a week. She also
attends lectures, movies, and concerts in the evening, and visits friends
who are infirm and runs errands for them. When she does not feel like
going out, she surfs the web and keeps in touch with relatives and friends
through email.

To hear of all her activities, you would assume that Joan is in tip-
top shape physically but this is not so. She has a significant hearing loss,
difficulty seeing, a torn rotator cuff and pain in her knees. But her attitude
keeps her young and active: an attitude, I believe, that has been shaped
by the many challenges and changes she has faced, the transitions she has
experienced, and the adaptations she has made in her life, which began
in Germany in 1923.

My son-in-law introduced me to Joan by giving me a copy of the
first volume of her memoirs, *Chance and Choice: My First Thirty Years*,
written in 2007. She published a second volume in 2009, called *Change
and Challenge: My Life After Thirty*, which describes her life up until age
seventy. She is a close friend of his mother's in Buffalo, he told me, and a
remarkable person. He was so right.

When Joan was ten, Hitler came into power and her existence changed
dramatically from that of a carefree child to the restricted and fearful life
of a Jewish girl. Named Irmgard at birth, Joan wanted to join the BDM
(Union of German Girls) like many of her classmates, but she was not

allowed because she was Jewish. In fact, the kids often threw stones at the Jewish children. In time, she was forced to transfer to a separate school for Jewish children, which she attended from the time she was eleven until she reached the eighth grade at fourteen. When her best friend, a Protestant girl, told her she could not play with her any more, they both cried but found a hiding spot in the woods where they met secretly, for a little while.

Five years later, her family fled Germany for Birmingham, England leaving behind their friends, their dog and three parakeets, as well as a large house and garden, and a comfortable way of life. As a refugee, Joan was able to get a scholarship to a prestigious girls' high school so she could continue her education. It took her awhile to adjust socially, especially since no one could pronounce her name. She decided to change Irmgard to Joan, the most popular name in her class. It allowed her to camouflage herself so she would fit in with the other girls. Because they thought heavy bombing would ensue in Birmingham, the authorities evacuated all the school children to the country. They stayed there a year but no bombing occurred. When the students returned to the city in 1940, the bombing started up. Joan and her parents shared a bomb shelter with an English family.

I hated leaving my bed just when I was getting warm, so every night I took my homework and hot water bottle to the cellar straight after dinner and stayed there for the night. Mother kept her knitting there and used it to calm her nerves. Father was stoic and seemed quite relaxed. "Don't worry about the bomb you heard," he would say. "It didn't hit you." My father had survived the trench warfare of World War I as a corporal in the Kaiser's infantry; maybe that's why he was relatively relaxed!

It was a tense time: all Germans in the U.K. were designated "enemy aliens," even Jewish refugees. They had to report to a court where a judge decided each person's fate. Most were sent to internment camps. Fortunately, the judge allowed Joan's father to keep his job, at his boss' request, but her brother and his young bride were interned for a year, which destroyed their marriage.

Joan attended the University of Birmingham and earned an undergraduate degree in physiology. Meanwhile, the war raged on, so to do her part, she took a job at night assisting the air raid wardens by spotting incendiary bombs as they dropped. In 1949 she received her Ph.D. from Middlesex Hospital Medical School in London and continued her research as a post-doctoral fellow at King's College, London. In 1952, she married Peter Staple, a dentist in the British Air Force. Within a year she got pregnant, but it was a difficult time as eczema, which had plagued her for years, recurred, and she had to be hospitalized.

A few years later with their two young sons in tow, they moved to Birmingham, Alabama because Peter obtained a tenure track position as an Assistant Professor at the University of Alabama School of Dentistry. Three months after they settled there, Joan's parents died suddenly, following a car accident in England. She was devastated but they could not afford to go back for the funeral. Gradually, the true Southern hospitality shown by their neighbors and the Dental School faculty made them feel at home. Peter had doubled his salary, so they were much better off than they had been in England. But they never liked the heat and humidity.

It was a challenging time for them in other ways as well. Everywhere they saw signs reading "Colored Drinking Fountains" and restrooms for "White Ladies Only." The Klan had a large presence and that terrified Joan. Many Southern Jews kept a low profile but Joan wanted to get involved in the Civil Right movement. It was one reason why they joined the Unitarian Church.

I was active in the civil rights movement but I was also a Southern lady, a housewife just like in Betty Friedan's book, The Feminine Mystique. *When I got married, I thought that was the end of my career; I would be a full time housewife and mother. It did not occur to me that the children would grow up! Reading Friedan's book gave me the push I needed to get back to work. She made me question what I was doing sitting home all day.*

When Alabama Governor George Wallace "stood in the schoolhouse door" to block integration, Peter decided he had enough: he resigned his position and the family moved north to Buffalo, New York, where Peter accepted a professorship at the State University of New York and

Joan received a research position. That was a hard adjustment too. Other than Joan's cousin, no one made them feel welcome. But after seven years at home, getting back into the lab gave Joan the grounding she needed and she was thrilled to be able to continue her research on nuclear transplantation.

In 1973 at age fifty, growing tired of the constant hassle of writing grant proposals, she left the research lab and began a new career teaching at Canisius College, a Jesuit liberal arts college. After the initial adjustment—learning how to give assignments, schedule quizzes, grade on a curve, and even select her wardrobe—she enjoyed this new phase of her life. Besides teaching biology, she started several new courses, including the Women's Study Program.

It was not until Joan turned eighty that she felt her age. She began to lose her hearing, her eyesight grew problematic due to macular degeneration, and a torn rotator cuff rendered her right arm almost useless. Even after shoulder surgery (performed by one of her former students) she could not write on the board or even lift a coffee cup. A pain management specialist told her that the shoulder would never get better and she should just adapt. Not about to accept his prognosis or give up, she consulted a sports medicine specialist, who prescribed physical therapy, and her arm did improve.

Since she had problems seeing and hearing, she decided to stop teaching after thirty years in the classroom. Then knee pain due to osteoarthritis forced her to give up both downhill and cross-country skiing, her passions for years. That same year she and her husband, who had symptoms of early stage hydrocephalus, moved into a Continuing Care retirement community (CCRC) and she became his caregiver. All these losses catapulted one upon another. It was a depressing time and Joan knew she had to find a way to thrive. During the next eight years she developed a philosophy that has helped her cope with the many losses that are typical of her age group.

I live one day at a time and follow the Serenity Prayer: I try to know the difference between the things I cannot change and those that I can. I cannot completely restore my eyesight or my hearing, but I have been successful in getting hearing aids that work for me. I went to three different audiologists until I found one who prescribed the right ones for me. You have to keep at it. It's hard to seek help but you need to do it. Don't just scream and cry. I'm still trying to overcome my reluctance to ask for help.

Psychologists say "Do something you enjoy." Well, I can no longer do what I enjoy. For years I loved to ski and ride my bike. I cannot ski at all and it's getting harder and harder for me to cycle. I also loved reading, but I cannot see regular print any more. So I say, "Enjoy what you can still do." I cannot ski but I can still walk so I can enjoy the out-of-doors on a nice day. Thanks to Kindle, I can read books again by enlarging the typeface. It used to be impossible for me to have a conversation at parties, but now with my new hearing aids, I am doing fairly well.

So I have learned to count small successes. I have also learned to feel grateful for what I have. I write a "good blog" once a week about the things I'm grateful for. These are helpful to me because I can look back to see what I wrote a year ago to see if things are better or worse; this helps me keep things in perspective. Writing the blog also helps to counteract all the unpleasant things and control depression. A lot of people are worse off than I am. I'm grateful for my friends, my "3Cs" –car, cat, and computer— and good food. Just for little everyday things….

Out of my blog, I have developed what I call the Sour Grapes Theory. One day my therapist reminded me of all my wonderful memories. I told him, "I don't want to think about them. They make me miserable. I can't go back there." But then I remembered that it was not all roses. Everything was not always nice and that's how this theory developed.

Here's what you do: if you loved hiking (but can no longer hike), think of the blisters, sudden down pours, lurking bears. Tennis a favorite hobby in the past? Remember the missed volleys, tennis elbow, the klutzy doubles partner. Biking? Your butt aches and the wind is always against you. You get the idea. Sour Grapes helps me appreciate what I have today.

These ways of coping have helped Joan compensate for the losses that occurred in her eighties. She also used them when facing her husband Peter's death in 2011. I wondered, though, as she reflected on her longevity, in what ways she felt her early life experiences prepared her for living as an older woman.

I read a book recently that made a lot of sense to me. It is The Status Syndrome *by Michael Marmot. He says that people who age successfully do so because they have had considerable control over their lives as well as social support, which is more typical of persons of higher social economic status. He thinks this is more important than having a healthy diet, plenty of exercise, and good medical care.*

To some extent this applies to me. Although my family, while wealthy in Germany, was poor refugees in England, I did not really feel deprived: when World War II broke out everybody around me seemed to be poor. Food and clothing were rationed; there just was not much to buy even if you had money. Yes, I was cold and hungry, but no more so than my friends. I still had some control over my life: I could choose what to study at school and university and decide to move to London for graduate study. And I did have social support from family, friends, and colleagues throughout my early life.

I don't think I had a healthy diet as a young woman: I fried everything— it was quick and tasty. I probably did get enough exercise because I had no car, so I walked or biked everywhere. And we got good medical care under the National Health Service even in those pre-antibiotic days.

At age ninety, Joan Lorch Staple has developed a well-balanced approach to living that younger women can learn from. We can try to take control over our lives right now—both for what it can mean to us in the present and for how it will prepare us to live well in our eighties and nineties. We can do that by being as physically active as possible, nurturing strong relationships, and participating in stimulating activities. And we need to counterbalance that with acceptance: learning to live with the things that cannot change and to acknowledge our limitations as we age, whether that means following the Serenity Prayer or finding our own way to let go.

And there is something else you should keep in mind as a young or middle-aged woman: stay connected with your parents and grandparents while they're still alive. Visit them, write, email, phone. Although my family lives far away, my two sons and four grandchildren help me in many ways. They encouraged me to write my memoirs. They were always there for me when I needed them.

As I reflect further on Joan's earlier experiences, I wonder if she were my age again, would she have done anything differently to prepare for her later years? This is what she said,

I don't think you can prepare for your older years, but I would say to do as much as you can now. Don't retire too late. By the time I retired at eighty, Peter was sick and then we couldn't travel together. Go while you can. Try everything. Be active. And always do something different. At fifty, I started a new career teaching at a liberal arts college. That opened a whole new world to me.

Adaire Joy Klein, 81
An Observant Life

THROUGHOUT ADAIRE KLEIN'S LIFE, SHE HAS FELT a very personal obligation to fulfill the commandment from daily prayer: "to perfect the world under the sovereignty of the Almighty." Three times a day, she recites this prayer of *Aleinu* and accepts its obligation. She sees it as her personal responsibility and commitment to learn to live together with others in peace and harmony.

Being part of a community fulfills this commandment. In Adaire's case, community consists of her own large extended family as well as the community created by her work as the Director of Library and Archival Services at the Simon Wiesenthal Center-Museum of Tolerance in Los Angeles.

I met Adaire at the Center-Museum on a trip to Los Angeles in November 2012 at my publisher's suggestion. He told me that not only is she one of the leading figures in Judaic library life in the United States, but the *Jewish Journal of Greater Los Angeles* chose her as "Mensch of the Year" in 2007. We were only able to meet for an hour because of time pressures in both our schedules but then followed up with several telephone conversations. I was impressed by how her professional and her personal lives mesh, and by her resilience in adapting to transitions and tragedy by drawing on her beliefs and on the rituals she finds comforting and healing as an observant Jew.

Adaire was born in Leavenworth, Kansas, where her father, the son of a Russian émigré, worked as an associate warden at the federal penitentiary. They only lived there for two or three years because little opportunity existed for their family to practice its traditional Jewish ways. They could not buy kosher food or be part of a Jewish community, because no other

Jews lived there. Next they moved to Lewisburg, Pennsylvania for a couple of years and then ended up in Columbus, Ohio when Adaire was six and stayed until she graduated from high school. Her mother, who grew up on the Lower East Side of New York and on a dairy farm in Connecticut as the youngest of fourteen children, believed firmly in early childhood education; she opened a preschool in their home wherever they lived.

An event stands out in Adaire's childhood: a trip she took with her mother and brother to Texas in 1945, where her father was a USO director and lay chaplain during the last years of World War II.

Spending a few weeks in Texas was a strange experience. I was thirteen at the time and this experience had an impact on the paths I have taken ever since. We were on a train in the middle of the night. There were no seats, people were sitting on suitcases. The train stopped and in the middle of nowhere, the conductors went through the cars shouting, "All you niggers get out and move to car x." That memory has stuck with me all these years. It was not the experience I would have had in my own home. In Texas, African Americans would cross the street when they saw us coming, because they were not allowed to pass a white person on the street.

When I came back I noticed in junior high and in high school that we had little or no social mixing of black and white students. It did not bother me because my closest friends happened to be black. They were welcome in my home. My parents would never dream of saying "no" but as I look back, I realize that the separation was part of a bigger picture. At first, I thought, well, this is just Texas. Then, I thought, this is the South. But I came home and found that in my high school it was the same. It was all part of a bigger societal problem.

Adaire joined the second class at Brandeis University. Coming from a small Jewish community in the Midwest, she had no idea what lay ahead of her either academically or Jewishly. She was not prepared for the intellectual competition, the huge amount of reading, or the writing of term papers. At the end of the first quarter, she landed on academic probation. But by working hard, she remedied that by the end of the semester.

When Adaire entered Brandeis, she was not aware that the school offered different meal plans. One day, she noticed that most of the students with whom she ate were eating kosher meals. Her family kept a kosher home, but they did eat out, so when she decided to sign up for the kosher meal plan, this decision had broad implications for her.

What I did in my home was what my parents had established; I adopted that as I went into adulthood. The decision I had to make now was if I went on the kosher menu at school, it had to go beyond my life as a student. I could not accept being one way in school and one way at home. I struggled with this decision because it differed from my parents' practice at home; I felt that it was a new commitment in my religious observance. As it turned out, this became a turning point that ultimately impacted on my entire religious identity. As time went on, I became more observant in terms of Shabbat *(observing the Sabbath) and* kashrut *(Jewish dietary laws).*

While Adaire continued to develop friendships in her major, Hebrew literature, she was also playing matchmaker. One day her brother, recently discharged from the U.S. Navy, asked her to find a "girl" to write to him, saying that he would like to visit the campus. Her friend Teresa agreed to write the letter, her brother visited, and he and Teresa developed a strong correspondence. They were married a year later. At their wedding Adaire met her husband, but they did not date or communicate in any way for five years, partly because he was in the U.S. Army, stationed in Germany during the Korean conflict. She was also preoccupied with school and working part-time. Neither of them felt ready for a commitment. During this period, she did stay in touch with his family, however, and when he returned, he quickly proposed.

Adaire and Manny recently celebrated their fifty-fifth wedding anniversary. They had three children together: two daughters and a son. Their son died suddenly of complications from sleep apnea in 2009. They have fifteen grandchildren, ranging in age from seven to thirty-one; six great grandchildren, from six months to eleven years old, and two more on the way. Their daughters and their son's widow live in Jerusalem, Milwaukee, and Baltimore, respectively.

Adaire received her bachelor's and master's degrees in Near Eastern and Judaic Studies from Brandeis, teaching while she finished her coursework.

She taught afternoon Hebrew school and Jewish studies while she and Manny raised their family, first in New York and later in Los Angeles.

Manny was a broadcast engineer/technician at CBS for many years. When there was an upheaval at his job, they decided to move to California, taking advantage of a job offer by Adaire's younger brother. Because a Jewish day school existed in Los Angeles, they decided to move there.

My first job in California was filling in for a woman on maternity leave at a conservative temple. I taught there and realized that they had a marvelous synagogue library. I began to spend more time in the library, eventually working there part time. This brought back memories of working in the Brandeis library as a student. I enjoyed helping people do reference work and became active in the Association of Jewish Libraries (AJL). I also took Hebrew Union College and other evening courses so I could develop skills and knowledge in the library field.

Then in 1978, we heard there was going to be a library at the new Simon Wiesenthal Center, located in the same building as Yeshiva University of Los Angeles. They hired me to develop the library. I wanted the challenge of developing something from square one, and I had it!

92

The library began in the basement of the Center with fifty books; today it houses more than seventy-five thousand, thanks to Adaire's diligent work in acquisitions. When Holocaust survivors began leaving artifacts, Adaire realized that they needed to expand to include archival services, which she also oversees. A typical memento? A letter written by a Belgian Jewish teenager while on a deportation train to Auschwitz to alert her friends to what was happening. She threw the letter out the window of the moving train, someone picked it up, and eventually donated it to the library.

Adaire spends her days answering reference questions, working with archival material, processing donations, keeping alert to what's happening in the library world and Holocaust/tolerance world, and programming. Adaire also teaches a weekly class to prospective converts to Judaism.

Immersing herself in the Holocaust every day can be depressing, she acknowledges, but she also finds it uplifting.

It is difficult. However, living and working amongst Holocaust survivors and the "Righteous Among the Nations" who sacrificed themselves to save others, has been a constant inspiration to me. Their courage inspires us to work even harder in our attempt to teach, train, and educate others to also perfect the world in which we live. I also feel that if I can contribute a little bit to make sure this is a world in which a Holocaust cannot happen again, that is primary to me.

Adaire works full-time, maintains a kosher home, observes traditional religious laws, and belongs to a modern Orthodox synagogue where she sits on the Board. Modern Orthodox Judaism is a movement within Orthodox Judaism that attempts to synthesize Jewish values and the observance of Jewish law with the secular, modern world. Ever since her children attended a Jewish day school, she and Manny made a conscious decision to do what the school taught and they patterned their lives around what the children learned, an interesting and unusual step for parents. Their children, now in their fifties, still maintain the same observant practices and lifestyle.

These practices served her well following the death of her son Dov at age forty-nine and helped her cope.

The week we sat shiva, *one person after another came in: family and friends from all over as well as strangers. One woman's response was typical. She said, "I want to thank you. Your son gave my son his first job and taught him how to be a* mensch." *Manny and I have found comfort in memories, and in the warmth, love, and friendship that was visited upon us.*

We suffered the sorrow of the loss of a child. Dov was our only son; he was carrying the family name. Now Dov's son will continue the family name. It has been tough. The outpouring of support and love helped. But immersing ourselves in the traditions of our ancestors was so meaningful. When someone passes away, you commit yourself to some kind of learning, usually the Mishnah, *the first section of the* Talmud, *which is a collection of early oral interpretations of the scriptures. Studying these passages is considered to lead to the elevation of his soul. We all pray that the departed is bound to life eternal. We try to expedite the soul in its journey as it moves on to the world to come. Dov's memory becomes a blessing for all of us. It's now almost four years since Dov passed away and I'm still studying* Mishnah *with a friend. It is very comforting.*

Adaire talks to Dov's widow every week and is close to their two children, both of whom are now married. It was Dov who planted the idea that Adaire and Manny should not stay in Los Angeles as they age, because none of their children lives there. After much deliberation, they have decided to make *aliyah* (moving to Israel). At this writing, Adaire has retired from her position at the Simon Wiesenthal Center-Museum of Tolerance and they are planning to move to Israel. It has been a complicated and emotional decision, but one that Adaire feels will be for the best in the long run.

If I had my real choice, we would stay where we are. We have our home, our garden (Manny grows roses), and plenty of fruit trees in our small back yard. We would be happy here. But my husband has leg problems; he's had two knee replacements. I'm a breast cancer survivor. Although I have been cancer free for over seventeen years, once you have been there, you live with a certain amount of fear.

I have some difficulty with aliyah *because I am a woman and feel strongly about my Jewish identity and participation in Jewish life. Judaism has always been central to my life. In the beginning I strengthened my identity on my own. When I arrived at Brandeis, I embarked on a new road of Jewish identity, surrounded by many Jewish fellow students as well as faculty.*

I know that things are different in Israel than in my shul, *which is like an extended family. I'm leaving a busy life, working full-time. I'm blessed with opportunities to reach out to young people in the classes I teach to prospective converts to Judaism. Will this happen when we make* aliyah? *I do not know.*

Aliyah has been on the back burner for some time. We have two friends there moving into retirement communities. We did visit several places. We'll probably settle in Jerusalem because family and friends will come there; they might not come to outlying communities. We realized that it's better to make these decisions ourselves than leave them in someone else's hands.

Please God, it should work out. The current news of conflicts in and around Israel is disconcerting and frightening but we have to have trust that God is everywhere.

Uprooting herself and moving over seven thousand miles from home at her age cannot be easy. Adaire feels she owes much of her resilience and courage to the constancy of her faith and the rituals that accompany it.

In addition, she feels that what she experienced as a younger woman has prepared her for life now, particularly what she learned from her mother.

Times were tough, but my parents—may their memories be a blessing—taught us how to live our lives. I learned early in life from my mother who lost her hearing at a young age. When a doctor at the Mayo Clinic told her he did not recommend surgery, she asked, "How long will I live?" The doctor replied, "You have two choices: you can go home and get into bed and get a housekeeper for the children and wait to die, or you can go home and live each day to its fullest and be a part of this world and a productive member of society." I was brought up to live each day to its fullest.

My mother also modeled for me how to be a wife and mother of a family that moved frequently. Both my parents encouraged me to have all kinds of friends; they were not all white and Jewish, and they encouraged me to pursue my interests and make my dreams come true.

Even though Adaire is moving to the other side of the world, she does not feel alone, and she continues to feel comforted by the memory of her parents. No matter where they live, Adaire and Manny find a way to keep in touch with their children, grandchildren and great grandchildren. Phone calls and emails constantly fly back and forth. On the occasion of her eightieth birthday, the family made a birthday book for her and included eighty reasons why they love her, each contributing a few ideas. Most of them went to Los Angeles when the synagogue honored Adaire and Manny in March 2013.

I would like to think that my mother continues to smile upon me today and is pleased with what I have done with my life. From my mother and father, I learned the importance of education, of perpetuating Judaism and my heritage, of living each day to its fullest. I hope I have imparted to my community of family, friends, and Holocaust survivors those same values that have molded me into the person I have become.

Leah Kosh, 76
An Internal Journey

Leah Kosh's favorite aunt once said to her, "When you were very young I worried about you because you were too good." For many years, she was a good girl, a good wife, and a good mother. Like many women of her generation, she acted exactly as the 1950s society dictated a "real woman" should behave.

And yet she was not entirely comfortable with these roles—she did not feel as if she fit that model but was too emotionally unaware to do anything about it. She did not realize she had choices until many years later.

Leah's journey has been an internal one. It began with her growing up with criticism, not liking herself, and then responding to conflicts in a passive-aggressive way. Going to art school, coming out as a lesbian, and losing a partner of twenty-one years were significant transitions along her path. Her passions of making art, teaching, and reading helped her cope with these transitions, but it was not until five years ago, in her relationship with her current life partner, that she tackled head-on the issues that have plagued her for over seventy years. In several conversations, Leah shared her lifelong journey with me.

I met Leah through my mentor whose sister Linda is Leah's partner. They live in Santa Fe from November to May and spend the rest of the year in Seattle, where Leah's son, daughter-in-law and thirteen-year-old granddaughter live. Leah and Linda see them often: they take trips together, babysit their cat, and celebrate each other's birthdays when they're in the same city. Leah sees her daughter less often because she is on the East Coast but they keep in touch by phone and email.

Leah welcomed me to the beautiful adobe house that Linda renovated and showed me her studio, her artwork, and their quiet, secluded garden. Then we sat down and talked over herbal tea.

Leah remembers that she had a reasonably happy childhood growing up in North Philadelphia in a middle class family. Her father owned a grocery store and her mother worked as a homemaker. Her grandparents lived nearby so were part of her extended family. She loved to read and sing and dance and remembers that she and her younger sister used to sing Yiddish songs as well as numbers from musicals and operas when they washed the dishes.

I remember my grandmother saying, "Oh you should have singing lessons and I'll pay for them because you sing better than Roberta Peters." I knew who Roberta Peters was and that was part of the problem in my family: either under praise or over praise, so it was very hard to figure out what reality was. I knew I did not sing like Roberta Peters, so where along this continuum was I?

Although situations like this left Leah confused, criticism was the more common response. In retrospect, she believes her family had the best intentions: they wanted her to be happy, but the criticism did not feel good at the time and had lingering effects.

I was hypersensitive, so I took in the criticism more deeply than someone else might have. As a teenager, I didn't like myself; I thought I was ugly, that something was wrong with me. I didn't fit in with my peers. I became mean to my mother in passive-aggressive ways. My parents did not model open discussion; things were not talked about. Especially being Jewish, there was a cultural paranoia among many Jews of my age: a sense of waiting for the other shoe to drop. To feel more secure, my parents surrounded themselves with Jewish friends rather than having a variety of cultural experiences.

When Leah went to Tyler School of Art at Temple University in Philadelphia, her narrow, prescribed world expanded. She was able to explore many different disciplines in art and academics, learn new ways of seeing and thinking, and experience different types of people, both professors and students. Because she could not select a major until her junior year, she took a wide variety of subjects: print making, sculpture, and drawing as well as dance and music. She loved being surrounded by such interesting, like-minded people. At Tyler, she had a close friend who mentioned that a female acquaintance had an interest in her. Leah was so naive that she did not know what she was talking about. She had a feeling of being both repelled and attracted and curious. Nothing came of it. She remembers Tyler as a "joyful experience."

At age nineteen, Leah married her drawing and painting professor, who came from a Ukrainian Eastern Orthodox family and was eleven years her senior. He was the father of her son and daughter. When their children were seven and eight, they spent a year in Rome while he directed the Tyler/Rome program, which was an extension of the school's main campus. It allowed juniors and first year graduates to study abroad for one year. Besides giving students a studio, they studied art history, English literature, and science.

Rome was the best of times and the worst of times. I knew that I was a lesbian before I left. At thirty-five I fell in love with a woman—a brief affair. It began to feel right that I preferred women.

So, I went to Rome as a married woman but I knew that we were not staying together. My husband was a good person and a wonderful father. I admired him, put him on a pedestal, and then tried to tear him down because I could not stand the discrepancy between how I saw him (superior) and how I saw myself (inferior). Neither view was accurate.

I had another motivation for going to Rome: I wanted an M.F.A. Before I left, I was making art while home with two kids. The admissions person told me in a nice way, "We know you have been making art but you're a housewife. Tyler is so selective in its graduate program. You should start in Rome because it's easier." I did just that. I shared a studio with another student, who happened to be on the committee to decide who got in for grad work. I found out that two hundred thirty applied, thirteen were accepted, and mine was the only one that was unanimous. Needless to say, I got my master's degree.

Leah's husband told her parents that she was a lesbian. When they questioned her at a later time, she told them it was true, but because her family did not talk much or express their emotions, she did not know how they really felt. They seemed to accept her partner at that time and included her in family gatherings. Her husband, on the other hand, was very angry when she came out and did not speak to her for thirty years, other than to make arrangements for the children to visit him.

In fact, Leah did not get a divorce until years later because their divorce was tied up with property and they could not make equitable agreements. After she graduated, she moved to center city Philadelphia where she made art and taught. She began a second lesbian relationship; this one lasted six years. After a few years together, her partner grew bored with Philadelphia and thought that Seattle would offer better opportunities, so they moved there in 1979, along with Leah's son. Her daughter received a four-year scholarship to a boarding school in Massachusetts and stayed on the East Coast. After two years in Seattle, Leah and her partner broke up but they have remained close friends.

Leah's life was transformed when she realized that she was a lesbian. She explained how she felt:

The transition from being a married woman to coming out as a lesbian was difficult. Not because I feared coming out but because I feared that our two children would be taken away from me. I even went as far as having brief relationships with two men so that I "passed" for straight. I did keep my kids and after the divorce was able to be out and have relations with women.

Initially, being lesbian created a whole new world for me. I met strong, independent women, hated all men for a while (converts are the worst kind). Choosing to love women changed my relationship to myself and therefore to the world. I felt stronger as a woman, more independent, and more at ease with myself.

It was like coming home. It's as if you have been in the wrong skin for too many years and initially you didn't even know that the skin didn't quite fit. And then you realized and chose a form that fit better and was more in keeping with your emotional and psychological state.

Finding out that I was attracted to women was one of the more liberating things in my life. It's like when you find something new. I was so excited about feeling the way I did. I read a lot of feminist books, I identified with the movement. In 1993 I was part of the Seattle group that joined the March on Washington, D.C. for gay rights. It was an exciting time. I never had any problems coming out because I did not realize my preferences until later in life and was not a gay adolescent in the fifties when it was considered a disease. In retrospect what I have come to understand is that my deep emotional attachments were always toward women.

Despite the new degree of comfort I felt with myself and with another woman, I was still unable to speak my mind when I was angry in intimate relationships. That would come later when I met Linda. I was still terrified of anger—of expressing it or having anybody express it to me—and therefore, created a lot of silence. These dynamics played out whether I was with men or women.

The move to Seattle was a difficult one for Leah because she did not have work for the first year, but once she started teaching, she felt at home. She taught for twenty-two years, teaching art to kindergärtners, the homeless, teenagers, college students, and seniors. At the same time she was making art and showing her paintings in Seattle galleries, which helped her establish herself there. She also found a new partner, Amber.

My teaching gave me the opportunity to express the strongest, most mature part of myself. The two areas where I have undeniable confidence in myself are in teaching and painting. I can be funny, compassionate, firm, and loving in teaching. I have gotten enough positive feedback and rewards in both fields to let me know that the outside world respects what I do.

My paintings have always reflected my inner emotional journey. Another escape hatch, they allow me to express rage, joy, confusion, and an ongoing interest in reconciling the disparate parts of myself.

My paintings most often explore the idea that there are a multiplicity of realities mutually coexisting and that these realities are our shadows and our mirrors— always with us, rarely acknowledged. The works are meant to evoke and provoke different emotional and psychological states, from playful humor to more complex feelings. They often combine non-objective elements with more recognizable images as a way of merging these things perceived as separate.

Leah only stopped teaching because Amber, with whom she had a twenty-one-year relationship, developed lung cancer. She chose to take time off to be her primary caregiver.

Amber was the first person close to me who died other than my parents, so that was the first time I experienced grief. I was very curious about what the grieving process would be like for me, so I kept a grief journal for a year. Sometimes the pain was not so great; then something would hit me and I would experience a fuller period of grieving. It was like waves on the shore, eventually getting smaller and smaller. At that point, I was not teaching but I read a lot, and I was able to paint. Painting has always been my way of expressing deep emotional feelings. Since at that time it was difficult for me to express anger, pain, and fear in words, painting was the vehicle through which I expressed these feelings.

I read a lot of Buddhist work. It helped me come to terms with Amber's death more easily by putting it into a larger context of change, cycles of birth and death, and acceptance of what is rather than what we might want. The teachings also opened a spiritual path for me that felt right at the time.

I have always been drawn to spirituality of one sort or other. I could never call myself a Buddhist; it just did not fit. I am a Jew—a cultural Jew. As a child, I went to a Yiddish camp sponsored by the Workmen's Circle (an organization committed to social justice, Jewish community, and Ashkenazi culture). Around the time of Amber's death, a Persian friend asked me to go to a particular synagogue because the music was so great. The rabbi talked about the importance of the silence between words. Afterwards I went up to him and said, "For a Jew, you make a good closet Buddhist." He responded, "It's not so closet." I went to that synagogue for years. It filled a spiritual need that I had because he focused on the Kabbalistic aspects.

Leah feels the relationship with Amber was a good one, but on reflection, she realizes that they could not express their anger directly and hated arguing. Yet they were loving and supportive of each other. After Amber's death, Leah was content being alone. Five years later, she started feeling a little lonely, so reluctantly she tried an online site for women looking for women. With a handle of JewBuArtist, she reconnected with Linda, a woman she had known many years ago in Philadelphia who was living in Santa Fe.

It was bashert *(Yiddish for meant to be) and it's been magnificent! Linda is the love of my life. We knew it when first we met. Well, it took four years to recognize the truth of that statement. We had some very rocky times. I would never in my life—not in my family, not in friendships, not in any intimate relationships—partnered with someone who yelled, someone who said exactly what she thought, someone who pushed me to be more direct and clear, and most importantly, someone who forced me to begin feeling my emotions when things got unpleasant.*

It was one of the most painful and joyful relationships I have ever experienced. Why did I stay? Because I was ready to look at the issues in myself (with the help of a wonderful therapist) that kept me from having a fuller, more mature partnership. Although I'm a lot better than I was at not avoiding arguments, not deferring, and speaking out even when I know I risk an argument ensuing, this acceptance of myself with all my imperfections, this inner freedom I now feel allows me to say at seventy-six, "It's never too late."

Leah's persistence in pursuing a healthier relationship is remarkable at an age when most people do not want to work so hard. Her physical health is good, some mild arthritis. In January 2010 she fell and smashed her elbow. That was a profoundly painful year—physically and emotionally. Due to a botched operation she was unable to move her fingers at all and could not raise her arm above shoulder height. She began painting with her opposite hand. A year later she had a second surgery to rectify the errors of the first one. This experience taught her to be more patient, to stop hating her arm, and to develop more compassion toward people in pain. She is still waiting for the nerve to heal completely but is grateful that she can paint with her chosen hand even though two of her fingers still lack flexibility.

Leah continues to explore her spirituality through reading and painting. She leads a quiet life but one filled with richness and depth. She begins her day with a morning study, reading and reflecting on books that provoke her thinking. Right now she is in the middle of Aviva Gottlieb Zornberg's book, *The Beginning of Desire: Reflections on Genesis*, a blend of literary insights and theological wisdom, derived from the author's lifelong immersion in rabbinic traditions and lore.

Leah also enjoys reading literary novels, mysteries, and Buddhist books. She reads an average of ten a month. Although she does not keep a traditional journal, she has kept a record of every book she has read since 1982. She finds it helpful to reflect on the type of book she read at a particular period of her life.

Leah spends the remainder of the morning painting. Often it is a "happy accident" that takes her to a surprising place in her artwork.

When I paint, that's my meditation. I'm sure any artist or most professional artists, if you have interviewed them, would say that the work comes through them. And that's how it feels because frequently I'll start out with an idea and I want to call it a happy accident or something beyond my higher self, whatever. It frequently ends up in a place of surprise to me. Or I'll look back, go through work that I have done and I have not seen for a long time, and I'll say, "Wow! Did I do that?" I didn't know I could do that.

I see my work evolving in a spiral. I start off with a realistic painting, then include more nonobjective stuff, maybe a previous way of working. To me, it's an organic way of painting. Will I ever stop making art? As long as I can physically do it, I cannot imagine not making it. It is my passion.

Leah spends the afternoons and evenings with Linda: walking, exploring, and going to cultural events. When I asked her to describe the best time in her life, she said, "This moment right now."

I wondered what advice she had for younger women so they too could experience that sense of gratitude for the present moment. This is what she told me:

Question everything. Look around to see how many options or choices you have. I didn't know I had options until I got to college. This was just the way it was. It's easier now. Stay open and listen to things you might think you cannot believe in. Other people's truths are true to them. Find your own truths.

And learn to like yourself. Find what's beautiful about yourself. Do not compare yourself to a media image. Look within.

Alice Kahn Ladas, 92
A Pioneering Spirit

ALICE KAHN LADAS LIVES IN AN INTERGENERATIONAL co-housing community in Santa Fe, where she maintains a private practice as a somatic psychologist. She serves on the staff of the Pastoral Counseling Center, plays classical music on the piano, and has written the lyrics and libretto for a musical play she hopes will be produced. She is a big part of the lives of her two daughters and three grandchildren. She also participates in the Senior Olympics, and in 2011 she played in the mixed-doubles tennis finals.

A pioneering spirit, Alice has not shied away from change or challenge, welcoming innovative thinkers into her life, even when they were unpopular or controversial. Twenty-one years ago, Alice leaped to prominence when she co-authored *The G Spot: And Other Discoveries about Human Sexuality*. The groundbreaking *New York Times* bestseller integrated the work of Freudians and sex researchers and brought female sexuality and satisfaction into people's consciousness. *The G Spot* has been translated into eighteen languages and sold more than a million copies worldwide.

While this was exciting, the relationships in Alice's long life have meant the most to her. Her mother served as her first role model, followed by Eleanor Roosevelt, whom she knew personally, and who taught her the importance of being politically active. Margaret Mead saved her thesis by joining her thesis committee. Other faculty felt that breastfeeding was not a worthy topic but had to support her because of Mead. Two men also had a big impact on her life: the gallery owner Sidney Janis, who was the father of Alice's first child, and her husband Harold Ladas, the father of her second child.

I first heard about Alice from my daughter, who is a good friend of Alice's Santa Fe daughter Pamela. At our initial meeting, Alice opened the door to her home and apologized. Her older daughter and grandson, who live in New York, had just left town and she was trying to get her home back in order. A petite woman with an athletic body, she moves briskly. Dressed in leggings, tall boots and a turtleneck sweater, she could easily pass for someone much younger. Her mind is sharp, she has a quick wit and she can be quite outspoken.

Once we settled in, Alice told me that she grew up on New York City's Central Park West, the only child of an interior decorator and a cotton merchant. Her parents divorced when she was two. Seeing her father twice a year—two weeks in Montgomery, Alabama and two weeks in New York City—allowed her to observe two different cultures. She disliked the way people treated Blacks in Alabama; in the North she had learned to honor all races. These beliefs led to her first job after college as Field Examiner for the Fair Employment Practices Commission. A case of hers is now in the Civil Rights Museum.

My mother was an interesting combination of very proper and very forward-looking. She loved giving fancy, formal dinner parties and would never allow a bouncing ball in the house, yet she had a sun lamp, so my friends and I could get our needed quota of sun during the winter. And she took me for an abortion when I needed one.

Although Alice's mother was born Jewish, she joined the New York Society for Ethical Culture as a young woman. Alice was not brought up as a practicing Jew or even as a cultural Jew or Zionist. The Ethical Cultural schools that she attended from kindergarten through high school influenced her thinking the most. These schools are based on the idea that living according to ethical principles is vital to living a fulfilling life, beliefs central to Judaism as well. After World War II, when many friends became more religious Christians and Jews, Alice became licensed as a Humanist Celebrant. She can legally perform life-changing ceremonies for those who prefer non-traditional experiences.

Alice received an elitist education for her day: She had music lessons at Julliard Undergraduate School, and went to Smith College, where she received a B.A. and a master's degree in social work. She received a doctorate in psychology from Teachers College, Columbia University. From the time of her graduation to the present day, however, her career—and her life—took some unconventional turns.

She became personally involved with Wilhelm Reich, a star pupil of Freud's who later became too radical for Freud when Reich set up sex clinics in Germany. Alice was attracted to Reich's inclusion of the body in therapy, and his interest in energy—how it gets blocked and how to release it. At the time most people considered an interest in his work radical.

Alice's interest in Reich led her to meet his student, Dr. Alexander Lowen. She helped Lowen form The Institute for Bioenergetic Analysis and to obtain his first publisher. Bioenergetics was the first somatic psychology in the United States to combine body-oriented therapeutic techniques with more traditional talk therapy. This is the type of psychology Alice practices today.

A major contribution of Lowen is that he worked with people standing up in addition to lying down and sitting. And isn't that the goal of all therapy? To get people to stand on their own two feet?

Alice's involvement with Bioenergetics led, indirectly, to her idea for *The G Spot*. In 1977, women in bioenergetic therapy began meeting separately from the men. Lowen believed in the Freudian view that mature women would be vaginally responsive. According to the sex researchers (and many women), this is not true for all women. Alice and her husband Harold, a professor of education at Hunter College, created a mail questionnaire so that female bioenergetic analysts could speak anonymously about their sexual experiences. These women reported that Bioenergetics had been helpful to them in many ways, but they also thought the clitoris was important and disagreed with Lowen's written view that man is woman's bridge to the outside world. Alice reported the results of that study at a meeting of the Society for the Scientific Study of Sexuality, where she met her co-authors to be, Whipple and Perry, who were talking about their research. The idea for the book on the G Spot emerged.

The G Spot was the first modern book to call attention to the existence of the Gräfenberg spot and discuss its location—an area of erectile tissue that can be palpated through the front wall of the vagina—as well as cover different types of orgasms.

While involved in the events of her career, Alice was also learning from her children and their fathers. Sidney, who lived nearby, filled the role of grandfather while Harold and Alice lived together with the children. Both men were involved with the family until their deaths the same year, 1989.

Sidney taught me to feel the grass under my feet, and to love art, tennis and dance. Harold taught me to finish cycles of action, how to lay bricks, to be at home in the ocean, to be patient. He helped me do my life's work with research on women and bioenergetic analysis and the G Spot. But that does not begin to answer the question of their impact on me.

After Harold died, Alice did not want to live alone in a New York apartment or move to a retirement facility. While covering an Omega Conference on Aging, she learned about co-housing and decided that was how she wanted to live. She looked around the country (there were only three at the time) and decided on the community in Santa Fe. At sixty-eight, she bought the property on which she built her present home.

People say Santa Fe is such a big change from New York, but I do exactly what I did in New York: I practice as a somatic psychologist, play chamber music, play tennis (with oxygen on my back), and work on my musical.
Sidney taught me to listen to the younger generations. The "kids" who live in this community—the "kids" in their thirties and forties—are cutting edge of their generation. They have taught me to be more positive and less critical and they keep me in touch with what's going on politically.

Alice is not one of those older folks who cannot sleep. She still needs a full eight hours and cannot as easily stay up all night as she did when she was younger. She takes good care of herself but it takes a lot more time than it used to. She takes vitamins, uses a low level laser if she has a pain, and is taking chelation therapy to remove heavy metals from her body. She does not eat junk or meat that's not organic and tries to drink a fresh green juice daily. Because she had a blood clot, she uses oxygen when playing tennis or snowshoeing at seven thousand feet. It is not needed at sea level.

What does Alice think contributed to her longevity? At nineteen, she met the woman who almost became her mother-in law; she taught Alice about vitamins and the importance of organic produce.

I started doing yoga with Lilias (Folan) and exercise with Jack LaLanne on TV when the children were little. I played tennis and did a lot of dancing. I never smoked—I couldn't inhale. I tried pot but couldn't inhale that either. The fact is, I have been lucky: I feel good, I sleep well and I still exercise. I have not had a major accident or a major health problem. I have not been run over by a car. I was not at the twin towers when they fell.

From the time I was a small child, I was energetic and interested in many different things. My high school yearbook said, "May you keep up your usual varied activities in your usual spicy way" and that holds true today. I was born with good genes even though my parents died young, and I'm enjoying a healthy, active late life.

Although Alice has not changed much physically in recent years, she feels she has shifted in other ways: she has more perspective, is less reactive, and a bit more understanding. She feels like she is in her sixties or seventies and believes she has more in common with that age group. But most people do not see her that way.

People in my community tend to identify me with their parents, and that is a bit isolating. I don't fit in with the typical ninety-year-old's interests. It would bore me to go to an exercise class for old people. It's a bit lonesome at times, though…Most of my good women friends are dead or ill, which is what happens if you live for so long.

I do not feel sorry for myself. I am really lucky to be alive and able to participate in the lives of my children and grandchildren. And lucky to still be able to work and play.

Although a humanist, Alice is not very proud of the human race. Greed and power seem to still be the major motivations. She is very concerned about what is happening to the planet and sad over all the species that are becoming extinct. If the human population continues to grow and demand an ever supposedly higher standard of living, she believes, there is no way to save the oceans and forests.

It's a scary time. I don't know whether we're going to succeed and save humankind. I think the planet might survive and I would like my family to survive. Is the human race headed for extinction? I wonder what Mrs. Roosevelt would think if she knew what we are facing politically today? It's a difficult time to be old and aware.

I'm concerned for my grandchildren. Our family lives in two of the three most dangerous places in the country: New York, Washington state, and Santa Fe because of its proximity to Los Alamos Lab. My grandkids might not have the good life I had. That really scares me. I would like them to have a decent place to live with clean water, clean air, and healthy food, and I do not know if they'll be able to.

If the population continues to grow, I worry we'll have wars over water and food. It's amazing to me that people don't understand this. People don't know that you can't have the population exploding and all live like upper class citizens of the United States.

112

These big issues occupy Alice's thoughts. With that in mind, I wondered what advice she has for younger people to help them prepare for their later years.

Pay attention. Do not dwell on past mistakes but learn from them. Here is an exercise I give my clients: Write down your goals fast—what would you like to have happen in the next three months, in the next five years, and if you're going to die, in the next six months. And then pick the three most important things and write what you would need to do to accomplish them. I do that myself twice a year. Sometimes my list is too long and I have trouble prioritizing the items.

I would also tell younger people to pay attention to their bodies. If you have experienced traumas, work them out. Do not bury them. Give your body what it needs, whether it's emotional or nutritional. You only get one body.

Looking back on her long life, Alice says it was exciting to have children, to write a best seller, and to make a mini–contribution to her field. She felt gratified last year when she received a medal as a distinguished alumna from Smith College, which was a very conventional institution when she attended it. Today it is much more inclusive and progressive.

The president of Smith asked a question of the five of us who received medals. When no one answered it, I said, "I'll take advantage of this opportunity. When touring for The G Spot *book, our publicist said you do not have to answer the question you're asked." Everyone roared. So I said, "I want everyone in this room to go home and call their senator to rescue Planned Parenthood." The place erupted in applause. I continued, "See this water bottle. It has a built-in filter. I never have to buy a plastic water bottle again." They all erupted in applause again. Then I said, "I want you all to take good care yourselves so you can take care of the planet so my grandchildren will have a safe place to live." The place erupted again.*

That's where I'm at today... still being a pioneer. It happens to me in spite of myself...It's not comfortable. It can be lonely and contentious. But I can't seem to help it. I'm still totally involved in life on so many levels. That's where my interest lies. So I wear my ET pin and live with the belief that we are probably not alone in the Universe.

114

Esther Altshul, 89
Matriarch and Mensch

THROUGHOUT THIS BOOK WE HAVE OBSERVED THE many ways that older women live their lives with vitality, meaning and passion. We have seen their various connections with Judaism and sensed their deep love and affection for their grandchildren. The meaning of the grandmothering role and how it meshes with the other roles in their lives, however, has not been explored. Esther Altshul, the matriarch of a large extended family, typifies many new grandmothers. Becoming a grandmother has given her renewed strength, joy and confidence later in life, building on the solid foundation set in her early years.

I became aware of Esther when I met one of her sons and his wife on a trip in the winter of 2013. When her daughter-in-law heard about the book I was writing, she immediately urged me to include Esther. "Grand-parenting has brought her into her own and changed her life," she told me. "She has given so much to the family, and gained so much herself."

Born and raised in the Chicago area, Esther grew up in an affluent, liberal, well-read family in Wilmette, on the North shore. Her father worked in advertising and her mother in social work. She had both an older and younger sister and they all loved their annual trip to Boulder, Colorado every summer where their parents took courses at the University.

Although both of her parents were born Jewish, her mother was the driving force in regard to religion; her father went along. She was active in Hadassah, personally knew Harriet Szold (the founder of Hadassah), and helped form the first synagogue in the Chicago suburbs. At home, they often lit candles on Friday nights and always had a Passover Seder.

Esther's mother was pleased when Esther married "a nice Jewish boy," whom she met through a mutual friend at the University of Chicago. Gil received a bachelor's degree in economics when he was nineteen, and went on to meteorology school when World War II broke out, serving as a meteorologist in the Pacific. Esther was pregnant before he went overseas, and their eldest son was a year and a half old when father and son finally met. They had three other sons before she turned thirty.

I always wanted boys. I knew I would not be good at handling girls. I was not comfortable with feminine things, knowing how to shop, being domestic. I always felt at ease with boys and loved having a house full of them running around.

Gil worked for an instructional film company for a few years and then started his own company in the living room of his Highland Park home. Esther worked in the educational film division of the company. Initially she did the administrative and organizational work; later she produced educational films on women's health, early education and other topics.

I had to face a lot of challenges. I had to deal with five strong personalities. I was always the softer one who helped things run smoothly. We never had enough money or enough time. These were the challenges of having a large family and building a business. We did that successfully, the boys turned out well, and my husband cared for me until the day he died. That gave me the floor on which to build the rest of my life.

Gil died in his sleep at age sixty-one. The next day he was supposed to direct a film she was producing. He seemed to sense that his time was limited; he had bypass surgery six years before and had recently updated his will. Esther was not aware of the preparations he had made.

I was in shock. Here I was: a widow at fifty-eight. Now I recognized he had all the warnings and had prepared for it. There was no question he knew he was on borrowed time. I'm not someone who looks back; I tend to look ahead. When he was gone, I knew I had to move on with my life. The week after he died, I went back to work at the company. My family gave me a lot of support.

Esther stayed at the company for seven more years, working with her son who took the reins when his father died. Her family and friends helped her get through this transitional period. The year after Gil's death, she sold their rambling house and bought a condo in Wilmette, a mile from where she grew up. She lives with luxuries that she never thought she wanted but has come to enjoy. At age sixty-five, she retired. It took her awhile to adjust to a non-working life.

Facing retirement was a challenge. I was frightened of not working. I had been working for so long, I was not sure how to use my time. It took awhile to feel that what I was doing was meaningful. I never plunged into organizational work. I took a lot of courses at Northwestern and traveled with Elderhostel. Later on, I took trips with my children and grandchildren, and in the last seven years, have traveled with one set of friends, a younger couple. We have been everywhere. I also travel to see my children and grandchildren for holidays and birthdays. I play more bridge, which I enjoy a lot.

But I have had my share of health challenges as well. I have had three hip replacements, a mastectomy, and a knee replacement. I make a point to get into the pool every day for Aqua Aerobics to treat chronic, painful arthritis. From this ritual, I have built relationships with my swimming friends. They have varied backgrounds, are old and young, of different races and religions, and we have become good friends.

Becoming a grandmother changed her life and gave her a focus for her retirement years. Her daughter-in-law reflects on how this role evolved:

My thought about Esther is that she initially found the role of mother a challenging one and struggled with her identity. When she first became a grandmother, with our first born, she was not ready to be called Grandma and so we called her "Poppa Essie." After her husband died, she seemed to turn to family, especially her grandchildren for support and focus.

Over the past thirty years, she has prioritized her relationships with her grandchildren and has a unique relationship with each one. She has been very generous to them and gets a great deal of pleasure and satisfaction in this role that she seemed to grow into. Somehow her relationships with her grandchildren have helped her claim a sense of identity and worth. As is often the case, she seems more comfortable as a grandmother than she did as a mother.

After two grandsons, her first granddaughter was born and became the daughter she never had. They always had a special bond, were on the same wavelength, and to this day, talk about everything. Her last grandchild is also a girl. Her relationship with each of her seven grandsons has a special flavor as well.

I'm close to all of my grandchildren. They trust me, and our relationships are meaningful. If they say something is confidential, I keep it that way...When I'm with my grandchildren, there is never an awkward moment. We simply enjoy being together. I make a point of going to the West Coast at least twice a year to see the kids who live there. They tell me, "I feel real good when I'm with you." There is no question that I am closer to my grandchildren than to my children. It was different when I was raising my four boys: we were struggling all the time, I was dealing with a husband who was under considerable stress and had a very strong personality. And yet now, I'm at ease with my sons and their mates, too. In general, I am who I am and I like being that way, and people respond to that. I'm genuinely interested in their lives.

Esther likes living alone but she thrives on company. Her condo has become a center not only for family but also for her friends and their children.

This life is wonderful. Because my son sold our business profitably, I now feel I have enough to live on comfortably. I never felt that way before. This condo has become the center of my life. I lost two young friends to cancer, and I was able to educate their kids; I took them all the way through college. It's a big extended family. I love to have people here and people like to come here. It's not fancy, but a place where babies crawl all over the floor, and kids can run around.

I get a lot of positive feedback from the people I spend time with. I know the way my grandchildren feel about me and I know the way my friends feel. I don't have a sense of anxiety—except for my health. My husband, who I loved dearly, was not always easy to live with. We had great highs and challenging lows. Now, I don't have that kind of situation. I live comfortably, but I don't spend much on myself. I am able to put young people through school and help in other ways. I feel very good about that.

118

I'm no longer a career woman. That was another life. I don't think I have ever been as comfortable with myself as I have been in the last few years. I get my strength from the fact that people like being with me. That's a source of joy.

Her grandchildren and great grandchildren enjoy being with her and she thrives in the role. Now that her grandchildren are older—they range in age from twenty-three to forty years old—their relationship with Esther has changed.

My grandchildren are like friends. I'll have a drink with them and talk. Or I'll call them on a Sunday morning and catch up. I don't feel the age barrier, but then I have close friends of all ages. That's what sustains me. I'm comfortable with who I am. I'm not trying to compete or dress better than others because it's not who I am.

Part of what draws her grandchildren and great grandchildren to Esther must be her positive attitude, a quality that she feels has also contributed to her longevity.

I have a positive nature, which I probably received from my parents who were very forward-looking people and transmitted that quality to us. You just go on, like I did after my husband died. You don't dwell on what's wrong. You look at what's right. My father lived into his early eighties. Was that luck or good genes? There are so many ways to deal with older age. Do you need a walker? Would you like a driver? A Lifeline? These options are available to me, and I will use them when it's time.

Of course, it's very painful to lose good friends. On the other hand, it's a part of life. Many of my friends in their nineties will pass away. The hardest is to have young friends die. That seems wrong. It's out of order.

Being a people person, Esther has some advice for younger women on the importance of nurturing relationships.

Give as much time and thought to other people as you can. Be as optimistic as possible. Stay engaged with others and try not to isolate yourself. Reach out to others but do not expect much in return. You'll get more than you give. Today I'm going to a friend's house to play scrabble. What do you like? If you love books, start a reading group. If you're a swimmer, find others to swim with. If you like bridge, round up others to play with you. And then become part of each other's lives.

Esther has taken her own advice to heart: her life teems with family and friends. When she is not swimming, playing bridge, reading, or socializing, she enjoys her iPad and her iPhone. Many women her age are not computer literate but she thrives on it. She plays Scrabble, bridge, and other games. She keep up with the news, reads *The New York Times*, listens to public radio, and uses Wikipedia; and she texts, Skypes and does Facetime. And of course, she emails her grandchildren to stay in touch when she cannot see them in person.

As she approaches ninety, she has begun to notice some shifts in her physical self. She is not as quick as she used to be, she gets more tired than in the past, and sometimes she needs a nap. Although her friends tell her she still has a lot of energy, she feels that she has slowed down—but not as much as her friends who use canes and walkers and can no longer drive. In spite of the physical decline she has noticed, she feels good about the life she has created. "Being close to a large family makes life worth living," Esther told me. "I'm enjoying a wonderful old age."

Conclusion

I BEGAN THIS BOOK WITH THE NOTION THAT women who are adaptable and resilient live longer. I based this idea on research that proved that resilient adults "age more slowly, live longer and enjoy better health" as well as on my own intuition and experiences as a long-time observer and recorder of women's lives.

Upon reflection, though, the connection between resilience and aging raised more questions than it answered. I wanted to know what qualities contributed to women's longevity and what factors played a role in their resilience, how their earlier lives prepared them for life as an older woman, and what helped them adapt to change and transitions. I was puzzled about what made one person bounce back from tragedy, embrace life, and move on while another remained mired in depression.

It was only when I began researching this book and examining the lives of older women that I learned the many ways that resilience develops and how it can benefit women when they are younger as well as older.

From Estelle Bloom, the activist from Levittown, New York, I learned that the stability of a caring extended family and the affection of long-term female friendships gave her the confidence to speak out against injustices and the support she needed when tragedy struck. Adaire Klein showed me how her faith and its rituals as an observant Jew not only sustained her following the death of her son but also gave her the courage to make *aliyah* at age eighty-one. From Liz Norman, I observed how a passion can create resilience. In her case, every time she encountered difficulty or challenge, her love of learning—studying, reading books and taking classes—took her outside of herself, helped her cope with the issue at hand, and gave her the strength to move on with her life.

As I listened to the voices of the women whose stories I have presented in this book, I was struck by their energy, their accomplishments, and their modesty. Many of them insisted that they had led ordinary lives and did not deserve the recognition the book would afford them. This response was typical of this generation: women who put others first and who were raised to feel selfish if they made themselves a priority. When they read the completed chapter about themselves, they characteristically responded, "Thank you for making me look so good"—giving me the credit, rather than claiming their own experiences.

All of the women had some kind of physical problem or condition that developed as they aged, yet none let it interfere with her life. These conditions ranged from Parkinson's disease to chronic, painful arthritis to spinal stenosis; several were cancer survivors. None of them dwelled on these conditions in our conversations, or in their lives. They comprised a piece of their story but not a major focal point. Instead, they focused on the positives: their activities, their relationships, their passions, and their beliefs.

Ten Keys To Successful Aging

What can we younger women learn from the older women we met in this book? By reading about their lives, we can glean the qualities that have contributed to their longevity and their vitality. These qualities can be developed and nurtured—now. When cultivated at a younger age, they will prepare us for our later years and help us age successfully. Many of these very same traits also contribute to resilience, that essential feature we observed in all the strong older women in this book. Here, then, are the keys to vital, healthy aging:

1. **Stay involved and active.** Adopt a passion or cause you believe in. It will give you a reason to get up and get out. Remember what you enjoyed doing as a child. Revive that interest now. Expose yourself to new interests.

2. **Build a support system.** Avoid isolating yourself. Try to make new friends and include younger women among your friends. Make sure the support is positive; let go of relationships that are toxic or dragging you down. Join a bridge group or a knitting circle. Nurture your friendships, the newer ones and the long-term ones. Remember that you do not have to discuss everything with everybody. Part of maturity comes from knowing when to confront someone and when to let something go. Be forgiving of your friends.

3. **Take good care of yourself.** Stay active physically: exercise, hike, cycle, or do yoga or Tai Chi several times a week. Allow yourself to relax: take a nap or soak in a hot tub. Read a novel on a weekday afternoon. Eat healthfully.

4. **Continue to learn.** Take classes and seminars on topics that interest you. Keep your mind sharp by doing crossword puzzles or Sudoku or playing Scrabble. Join or start a book group. Travel in a way that fits your budget.

5. **Foster your creativity.** Take a painting, photography or ceramics class. Start piano lessons. Try new recipes. Plant a garden. Stretch yourself in new and different ways. Think out of the box. It's never too late to try something new.

6. **Develop a spiritual life.** Join a church or synagogue if that is meaningful for you. Develop a reverence for nature. Learn to meditate. Try to live in the present moment and appreciate it. Engender gratitude. Do this by keeping a gratitude journal; jot down what you're grateful for every day.

7. **Adopt a positive attitude.** View challenges and crises as turning points and opportunities. Recognize what you can control and what is out of your hands. See the glass as half full. Find alternatives to lost physical qualities. If you can no longer dance, then find a way to teach dancing.

8. **Cultivate generativity.** Explore ways to give back. Teach a subject you care about. Volunteer at a local shelter or other social agency. Mentor a young woman in your field. Tutor at a literacy center.

9. **Find yourself a mentor.** Get acquainted with a woman over seventy-five like the ones featured in this book who are leading dynamic lives. Volunteer at a senior center, read to someone, or teach an older woman a skill or hobby you have as a way of getting to know and understand her. This will help prepare you for your later years.

10. **Develop resilience.** Have emotional strength and flexibility for the unanticipated events in life.

The Privilege Of Aging

Throughout this book we observed the many ways that older women navigate their long lives and continue to thrive in their later years. Getting to know these women and working with them has been an honor. Meeting them has shifted my thinking as well. I can say with confidence that I no longer fear the years ahead. I now believe that the time after seventy-five is an active developmental period in which I can keep growing and learning—that's exciting! Having twelve role models—real women I know and admire—who are leading involved, productive lives has paved the road for younger generations. They have shown us how to live our later years with spirit, enthusiasm and meaning. Knowing the steps to follow to ensure a healthy, successful old age gives us a road map for now as well as for the future.

Adopting actress Laura Linney's words from the introduction, I believe that aging is a privilege, especially when you consider the many people who are not fortunate enough to experience it. It would be a pleasure for me to play tennis at age ninety-two like Alice Ladas or to debate politics with my grandchildren like Liz Norman at one-hundred-and-two. I hope these women will inspire you to take care of yourself so you, too, can experience the privilege of aging and age well.

Recommended Reading

Arrien, Angeles. *The Second Half of Life: Opening the Eight Gates of Wisdom*. Boulder CO: Sounds True, 2005.

Bateson, Mary Catherine. *Composing a Further Life: The Age of Active Wisdom*. New York: Knopf, 2010.

Berrin, Susan. *A Heart of Wisdom: Making the Jewish Journey from Midlife Through the Elder Years*. Woodstock, Vermont: Jewish Lights Publishing, 1997.

Blair, Pamela. *The Next Fifty Years: A Guide for Women at Midlife and Beyond*. Charlottesville, Virginia: Hampton Roads Publishing Co., 2005.

Borysenko, Joan. *A Woman's Book of Life: The Biology. Psychology, and Spirituality of the Feminine Life Cycle*. New York: Riverhead Books, 1996.

Ephron, Nora. *I Remember Nothing: And Other Reflections*. New York: Vintage, 2011.
_____ *I Feel Bad About My Neck: And Other Thoughts On Being a Woman*. New York: Vintage, 2008.

Friedan, Betty. *The Fountain of Age*. New York: Simon & Schuster, 1993.

Jacoby, Susan. *Never Say Die: The Myth and Marketing of the New Old Age*. New York: Pantheon, 2011.

Heilbrun, Carolyn G. *The Last Gift of Time: Life Beyond Sixty*. New York: The Dial Press, 1997.

Levine, Suzanne Braun. *Inventing the Rest of Our Lives: Women in Second Adulthood*. New York: A Plume Book, 2005.

Mazer, Gwen and Christine Alicino (photographer). *Wise Talk, Wild Women*. San Francisco: Council Oak Books, 2007.

Pipher, Mary, Ph.D. *Another Country: Navigating the Emotional Terrain of our Elders.* New York: Riverhead Books, 1999.

Rountree, Cathleen. *On Women Turning 70: Honoring the Voices of Wisdom.* San Francisco: Jossey-Bass Publishers, 1999.

Schachter-Shalomi, Zalman. *From Age-ing to Sage-ing.* New York: Warner Books, 1995.

Sheehy, Gail. *New Passages: Mapping Your Life Across Time.* New York: Random House, 1995.

The Transition Network and Gail Rentsch. *Smart Women Don't Retire—They Break Free.* New York: Springboard Press, 2008.

Tenneson, Joyce. *Wise Women: A Celebration of Their Insights, Courage and Beauty.* New York: Bullfinch Press, 2003.

Uphan, Emily W. and Linda Gravenson. *In the Fullness of Time: 32 Women on Life After 50.* New York: Atria, 2010.

Zackheim, Victoria. *For Keeps: Women Tell the Truth About Their Bodies, Growing Older, and Acceptance.* Berkeley: Seal Press, 2007.
_____*The Face in the Mirror: Writers Reflect on Their Dreams of Youth and the Reality of Age.* Amherst, New York: Prometheus Books, 2009.

About the Author

PATRICIA GOTTLIEB SHAPIRO IS AN AWARD-WINNING AUTHOR who has written or co-authored nine nonfiction books. She specializes in writing and speaking on the issues of women at mid-life and older.

She has written about how women constantly reinvent themselves after their children leave home, through their friendships, by coming home to their true selves, and in other important ways.

Ms. Shapiro has a master's degree in social work and borrows from that training to understand the human condition, particularly women's development.

She is a widely sought lecturer, writing coach and yoga teacher. She is available for talks about women at mid-life and beyond, and can be reached through her website at www.wisewomenalive.com.

RECENT AWARDS AND RECOGNITIONS

GAON BOOKS

Patricia Gottlieb Shapiro. 2013. *The Privilege of Aging.* (**Selected for Author's Network, Jewish Book Council 2013-2014**)

Ruth H. Sohn. 2013. *Crossing Cairo: A Jewish Woman's Encounter with Egypt.* (**Nominated for the Sophie Brody Medal, American Library Association; Selected for Author's Network, Jewish Book Council 2013-2014**)

Michael L. Kagan. 2012. *God's Prayer: the Sacred Task of Living* (**Best Book Finalist in Religion 2012, New Mexico/Arizona Book Awards**)

Mati Milstein. 2012. *My New Middle East: Inside the Israeli Conundrum.* (**Best Book Finalist in Political Writing 2012, New Mexico/Arizona Book Awards; Nominated Best Book Dayton Literary Peace Prize**)

Ron Duncan Hart. 2011. *Islam and Muslims.* (**Best Book Finalist in Anthropology 2012, New Mexico/Arizona Book Awards**)

Zalman Schachter Shalomi and Netanel Miles Yepez. 2011. *A Hidden Light: Stories and Teachings of Early ḤaBaD and Bratzlav Hasidism.* (**Winner Best Book in Philosophy and Thought 2012, New Mexico/Arizona Book Awards**)

Vanessa Paloma. 2011. *The Mountain, the Desert and the Pomegranate: Stories from Morocco and Beyond.* (**Best Book Finalist for Young Readers 2011, New Mexico/Arizona Book Awards**)

Patricia Gottlieb Shapiro. 2011. *Coming Home to Yourself: Eighteen Wise Women Reflect on Their Journeys.* (**Best Book Finalist 2011, New Mexico/Arizona' Book Awards**)

CPSIA information can be obtained at www.ICGtesting.com
Printed in the USA
LVOW11s1604171013

357417LV00015B/489/P